NEW iLearn ENGLISH

4

Student's Book

Gisele Aga
Patricia McKay Aronis
Renata Chimim
Tatiana Martin

Pearson

MISTO
Papel | Apoiando o manejo florestal responsável
FSC® C103535

The publisher would like to thank the following for their kind permission to reproduce their photographs:

123RF: 178; **Artsy.net:** 129; **Barchester.com:** 139; **Calvinandhobbes.com:** 125; **Cartoonstock:** 42, 95; **Dreamstime:** 12, 28, 29, 34, 52, 84, 99, 100, 145; **Gettyimages:** 54, 55, 66; **Istock:** 10, 16, 18, 21, 27, 30, 32, 34, 38, 39, 40, 41, 42, 44, 45, 46, 48, 49, 57, 59, 60, 61, 62, 63, 64, 66, 68, 69, 71, 74, 75, 77, 78, 80, 82, 83, 84, 87, 88, 89, 90, 92, 95, 96, 98, 99, 100, 101, 104, 105, 108, 110, 112, 115, 117, 118, 119, 122, 124, 125, 126, 130, 133, 137, 139, 141, 144, 150, 152, 154, 156, 157, 158, 160, 161, 162, 163, 164, 165, 166, 167, 168, 170, 171, 172, 174, 175, 176, 178, 179, 181; **Pagepulp.com:** 85; **Shutterstock:** 10, 64, 78, 100, 149, 151, 152, 161, 169, 175, 178; **Smartcitiescouncil.com:** 114; **Transitionbroad.com:** 98; **Universidade Yale:** 68; **Whitney.org:** 129

Illustrations

Istock: 13, 24, 26, 37, 49, 66, 70, 76, 84, 96, 99, 103, 128, 140

Printed in Brazil by Reproset RPPA 222127

NEW iLearn ENGLISH

4

Student's Book

Contents

Student's Book

The *New iLearn English* uses the PPP learning methodology. In the **Presentation** stage new structures are presented, in the **Practice** stage students will practice the new structures by means of controlled activities and with more interference from the teacher, so that during the **Production** stage they can use these structures for more spontaneous communication.

Opening Pages

Every unit starts with two Opening Pages containing:

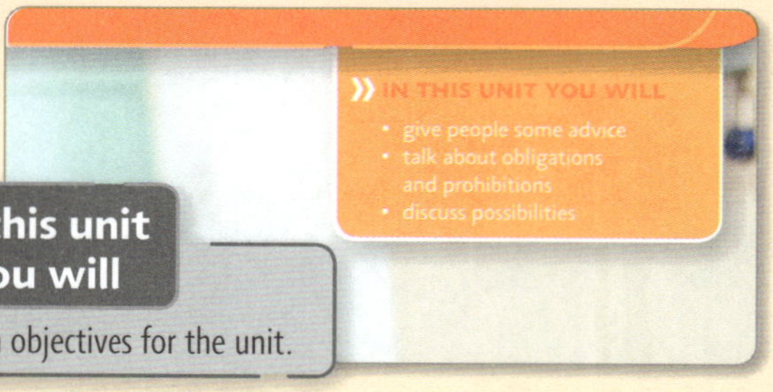
» IN THIS UNIT YOU WILL
- give people some advice
- talk about obligations and prohibitions
- discuss possibilities

In this unit you will
Main objectives for the unit.

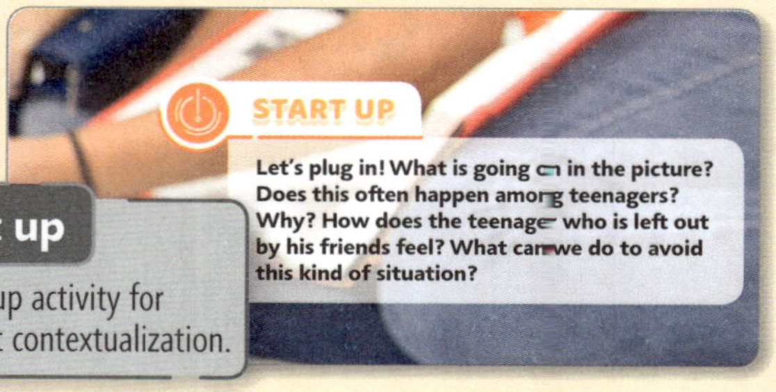
START UP
Let's plug in! What is going on in the picture? Does this often happen among teenagers? Why? How does the teenager who is left out by his friends feel? What can we do to avoid this kind of situation?

Start up
Warm-up activity for content contextualization.

LOADING
Section for the
Presentation Stage

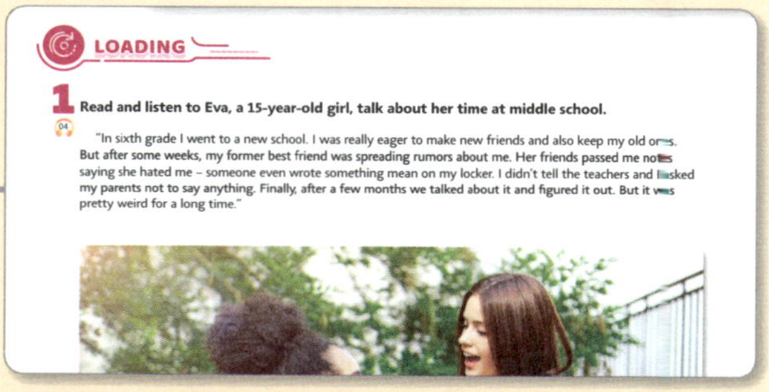
LOADING
1 Read and listen to Eva, a 15-year-old girl, talk about her time at middle school.

"In sixth grade I went to a new school. I was really eager to make new friends and also keep my old ones. But after some weeks, my former best friend was spreading rumors about me. Her friends passed me notes saying she hated me – someone even wrote something mean on my locker. I didn't tell the teachers and I asked my parents not to say anything. Finally, after a few months we talked about it and figured it out. But it was pretty weird for a long time."

UPLOADING
Section for the
Practice Stage

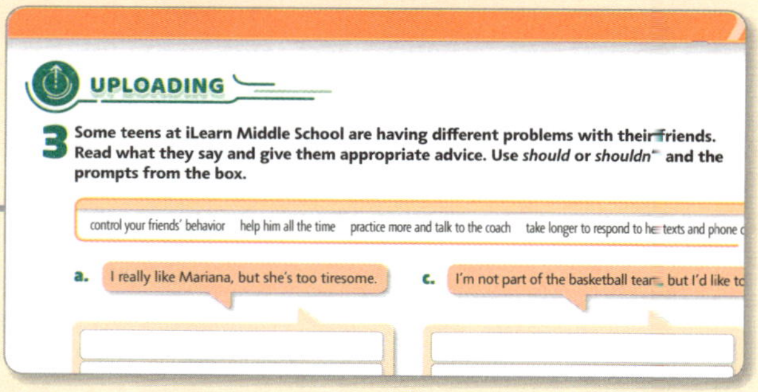
UPLOADING
3 Some teens at iLearn Middle School are having different problems with their friends. Read what they say and give them appropriate advice. Use *should* or *shouldn't* and the prompts from the box.

control your friends' behavior · help him all the time · practice more and talk to the coach · take longer to respond to her texts and phone c

a. I really like Mariana, but she's too tiresome.
c. I'm not part of the basketball team, but I'd like to

DOWNLOADING
Section for the
Production Stage

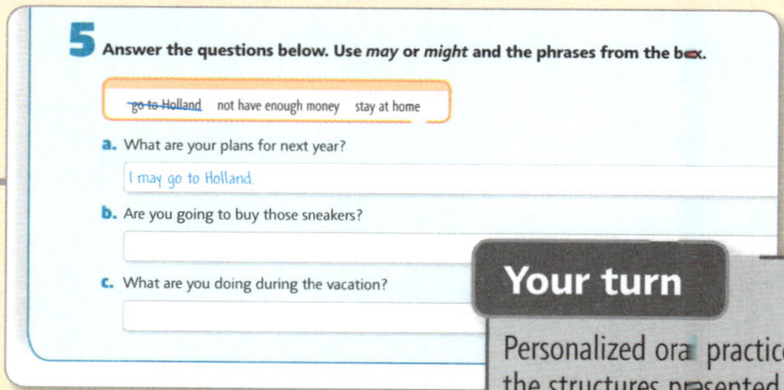
5 Answer the questions below. Use *may* or *might* and the phrases from the box.

~~go to Holland~~ · not have enough money · stay at home

a. What are your plans for next year?
I may go to Holland.
b. Are you going to buy those sneakers?
c. What are you doing during the vacation?

Your turn
Personalized oral practice of the structures presented.

iSkills

Integrated work focused on the four skills: listening, speaking, reading, and writing.

English for

Cross-curricular themes and vocabulary expansion.

rePlay

Revision of grammatical and lexical structures in a fun way.

Self-Assessment

Exercise with the main structures seen in the unit and feedback on performance (score).

Rewind

Revision of grammatical and lexical structures every two units.

Reading Hub

Extra reading activities with revision of grammatical and lexical structures in a fun way.

Workbook

Grammar Reference

Self-study guide for each unit.

iCan

Self-assessment of performance in the unit.

Digital Components

Pearson English Portal - Exclusive teacher and student areas for extra resources, including tests, audio, and e-books.

Welcome Unit

IN THIS UNIT YOU WILL

- review the use of the Simple Past
- review the use of the comparative and superlative forms of adjectives

START UP

Let's plug in! What did you do during summer break? Did you and your classmates do anything similar?

LOADING

1 **Maya's vacation was very special. She traveled with her family. Match her pictures to the correct description. Follow the model given. Number the sentences in the correct order (1-5).**

___ We arrived in the evening. Our first meal there was tambaqui, a delicious fish served with chestnut sauce. ___

___ In the afternoon we went to the fish market. They have all kinds of fish and a lot of different kinds of bananas. It was amazing. There, we said goodbye to Manaus. ___

___ After visiting Manaus we took a boat to Belém. In the boat there were hammocks where we could rest. ___

___ The next morning we went canoeing on the Rio Negro with a group of visitors from New Zealand. We saw many birds and I think I saw an alligator swimming next to the canoe! ___

a On January 3rd I started a wonderful adventure with my mom, my dad, and my brother. We took a flight to Manaus. 1

a.

b.

c.

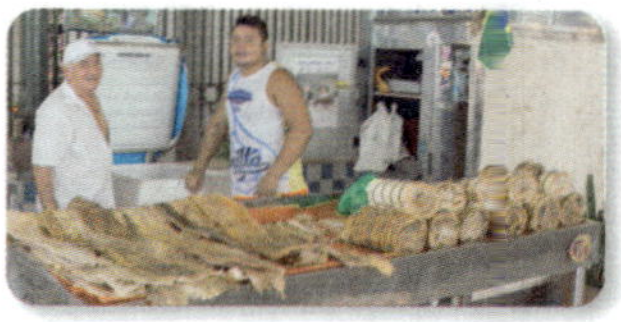

d.

e.

2 **Maya's classmates are asking her some questions about her vacation. Complete the questions and her answers with the verbs in parentheses in the Simple Past.**

Carlos: Which city did you prefer (you/to prefer), Manaus or Belém?

Maya: I preferred (to prefer) Manaus, but my brother ___ (to like) Belém more.

Bia: ___ (you/to sleep) on the boat?

Maya: No, I ___. I ___ (not/to want) to miss the view.

Ana: Where ___ (you/to stay) in Belém?

Maya: I ___ (to stay) at my uncle's house.

Rony: ___ (you/to eat) any other fish?

Maya: No, I only ___ (to eat) tambaqui. I also ___ (to drink) some delicious cupuaçu juice.

Grammar feed

Simple Past

Affirmative	Negative	Interrogative
Maya **stayed** at her uncle's house.	Maya **didn't stay** at a hotel.	**Did** Maya **stay** at a hotel?
Maya **flew** to Manaus.	Maya **didn't fly** to Belém.	**Did** Maya **fly** to Manaus?

Study this

Regular Verbs	Irregular Verbs
to stay – stayed	to fly – flew
to travel – traveled	to eat – ate
to arrive – arrived	to drink – drank
to start – started	to go – went

UPLOADING

3 **Write questions to these answers.**

a. Did you arrive in the afternoon ?

No, I didn't. I arrived in the evening.

b. What ____________________ ?

I ate tambaqui.

c. ____________________ ?

Yes, I did. I went canoeing in the Rio Negro.

d. Where ____________________ ?

I saw different kinds of fish at the fish market.

e. ____________________ ?

Yes, I did. I traveled by boat from Manaus to Belém.

DOWNLOADING

4 **Think of a place you visited and write a paragraph about your experience. Write where you went, when you went there, where you stayed, and what you did.**

LOADING

1 **In class, the students talked about their vacations. Now it's recess. They are talking about their school subjects for this year. Listen and read.**

02

Theo: Aagh! I am so annoyed! Math is the worst subject ever!

Mel: Hey! Why are you so angry? Today is only the first day of class. .

Theo: I know, but our teacher gave us a test today. Can you believe it? And, of course, Will got the best grade, and guess what? I got the worst one.

Mel: What? Teachers can't compare grades! If so, I would probably be the worst at history and the best at math.

Theo: She didn't compare them, but I wanted to know and asked everybody's grades. At least I am better at history than you, I guess.

Mel: Why do you compare grades? Honestly, I think history is more boring than math.

Theo: Math is the most boring and the most difficult subject. Geography is the easiest.

Mel: Of course you'd say that; your dad is a geography teacher! I bet he helps you!

Theo: Well, maybe sometimes...

2 **Read the dialogue again and circle *T* for Theo and *M* for Mel.**

a. This person had a test today. T M

b. This person is better at math than history. T M

c. This person is better at history than math. T M

d. This person's father is a geography teacher. T M

e. This person thinks history is more boring than math. T M

3 **Listen again and read the dialogue.**

03

Grammar feed

Comparative	Superlative
easy – eas**ier** than	the eas**iest**
difficult – **more** difficult than	the **most** difficult
boring – **more** boring than	the **most** boring

Study this

The exceptions are:

good	– better than	– the best
bad	– worse than	– the worst
far	– further/farther than	– the furthest/farthest

UPLOADING

4 **Complete the chart with the correct comparative and superlative form of the adjectives below.**

Adjective	Comparative	Superlative
cold		
big	bigger than	
young		
short		
intelligent		the most intelligent
beautiful		
expensive		

5 **Complete the sentences with the comparative or superlative form of the adjectives in parentheses.**

a. Mel is better than Theo at math. (good)

b. Matt is ______ in our class. (young)

c. In your opinion, what is ______ school subject? (easy)

d. I think geography is ______ history. (difficult)

e. This is ______ watch in the store. (expensive)

DOWNLOADING

6 **Write three sentences giving your opinion on some school subjects.**

a. ______

b. ______

c. ______

unit 1

You should respect her new friends.

» IN THIS UNIT YOU WILL

- give people some advice
- talk about obligations and prohibitions
- discuss possibilities

START UP

Let's plug in! What is going on in the picture? Does this often happen among teenagers? Why? How does the teenager who is left out by her friends feel? What can we do to avoid this kind of situation?

LOADING

1 **Read and listen to Eva, a 15-year-old girl, talking about her time at middle school.**

04

"In sixth grade I went to a new school. I was really eager to make new friends and also keep my old ones. But after some weeks, my former best friend was spreading rumors about me. Her friends passed me notes saying she hated me – someone even wrote something mean on my locker. I didn't tell the teachers and I asked my parents not to say anything. Finally, after a few months we talked about it and figured it out. But it was pretty weird for a long time."

2 **Read the text again and check (✓) the true sentence(s).**

a. The girl didn't want to make new friends at school. ☐

b. She changed schools when she was in the sixth grade. ☐

c. Her former best friend didn't care about her new friends. ☐

see word pop-up page 150

Grammar feed

Advice: *Should* - review

Friends **should respect** each other's new friends. Friends **shouldn't spread** rumors about each other.

UPLOADING

3 **Some teens at iLearn Middle School are having different problems with their friends. Read what they say and give them appropriate advice. Use *should* or *shouldn't* and the prompts from the box.**

control your friends' behavior | help him all the time | practice more and talk to the coach | take longer to respond to her texts and phone calls

a. I really like Mariana, but she texts me all the time!

b. Rob is constantly asking for help. I just don't have time for it.

c. I'm not part of the basketball team, but I'd like to be.

d. My friends are skipping class. I have to talk to them about that.

4 **Listen to Michaela asking for advice on a problem she is having with some friends. Then match the columns.**

05

a. She left school because

b. She will study at home until

c. Her parents work a lot, so

d. Her friends only talk about

( ) the new academic year starts.

( ) things like crushes and dating.

( ) she doesn't have anyone to talk to.

( ) she was bullied.

DOWNLOADING

5 **What advice would you give people in these situations? Write.**

a. My friends laugh at me because I don't have expensive clothes.

b. My best friend gets very bad grades at school.

Your turn!

Work with a partner. Read your pieces of advice. Are they similar to his/hers?

LOADING

1 Read and listen to these three teens talk about some school rules in their cities.

06

Hi! My name is Oliver. I'm from Auckland, New Zealand. I keep my hair long out of respect for my grandfather, who also had long hair. I'm a star student and athlete. I'd like to study at AC Grammar School, but my mom was advised I can't study there unless I cut my hair. Male students with long hair can't study there. The school has a strict grooming policy.

Hello! I'm Kate and I'm from Toronto, Canada. Halloween is next week and some schools in the city sent a checklist out to parents of DO's and DON'Ts for Halloween costumes. We shouldn't dress as stereotypes (such as terrorists or gypsies) or change the color of our skin, for instance. These costumes can be considered offensive. There will be Halloween parties at school, but we must watch out for what we wear.

Hi! My name is Huang Mei and I am from a small village in Beijing, China. I study in a school far from my village. Students from rural areas in China must move from their family homes and live in dormitories. They visit their families on weekends. Students who want to go to middle school must take an entrance exam in the last year of elementary school.

2 Read the texts again and circle T (true) or F (false).

a. AC Grammar School does not admit male students with long hair. T F

b. Students in Toronto are free to wear any kind of Halloween costume. T F

c. Students from small villages in China must live away from their family. T F

Grammar feed

Formal obligations and prohibitions: *Must* and *Must not*

Obligations	Prohibitions
We **must watch out for** what we wear.	We **must not dress** as stereotypes.
Students **must take** an entrance exam in the last year of elementary school.	Boys **must not have** long hair at AC Grammar School

Study this

Can = it's permitted

Must not = can't = it's not permitted

UPLOADING

3 **Use *must* or *must not* to write sentences about the poster.**

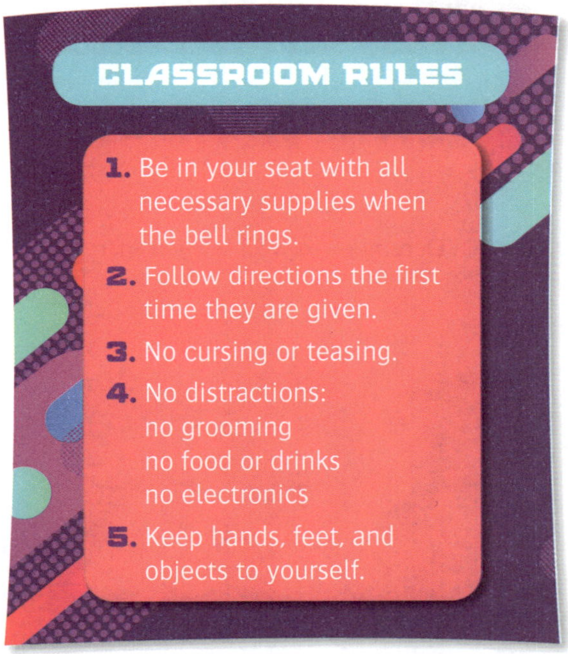

1. You must be in your seat with all necessary supplies when the bell rings.
2. ______________________
3. ______________________
4. ______________________
5. ______________________

DOWNLOADING

4 **What are some rules in your classroom? Write two rules using *must*, *must not/can't*, and *can*.**

a. ______________________

b. ______________________

Your turn!

Work in groups of three. Compare the rules you wrote. Are they similar or different?

LOADING

1 **Eva's father is being transferred to another state for work, so her family must move away. She is talking to some friends at school. Listen and read.**

07

Tyler: When's your last day at school?

Eva: Friday. I don't want to go. It's not fair.

Megan: Why don't you stay here with your grandma?

Eva: My dad said I have to go. He's afraid she might get too tired having a teen at home all the time.

Lily: We'll miss you, Eva.

Megan: Will we text each other every day?

Eva: Of course we will. I promise. Not all the time like we do now, but…

Tyler: Hey, cheer up! You might like the new school.

Eva: Yes, but I might not make friends there.

Lily: Oh, come on! You might come to visit your grandma in December, so we'll see you ther.

2 **Read the dialogue again and answer the questions.**

	Yes	No	Maybe
a. Is Eva happy about moving to another state?			
b. Is Eva going to stay with her grandma?			
c. Is Eva afraid that she might not make new friends?			
d. Is Eva going to visit her grandma in December?			

3 **Listen again and repeat the dialogue.**

08

Grammar feed

Future possibility: *Will* vs. *Might*

It's certain.

Affirmative Eva's friends **will miss** her.

Negative Eva **won't text** her friends all the time.

It's possible.

Affirmative Eva's grandma **might get** too tired.

Negative Eva **might not make** friends there.

Study this

will not → won't

might not → no contraction

UPLOADING

4 **Use the prompts, the pictures, and the information in parentheses to write sentences with *will*, *won't*, *might*, or *might not*. They can be affirmative (✓) or negative (X).**

a. clean her room on Sunday (It's certain. / X)

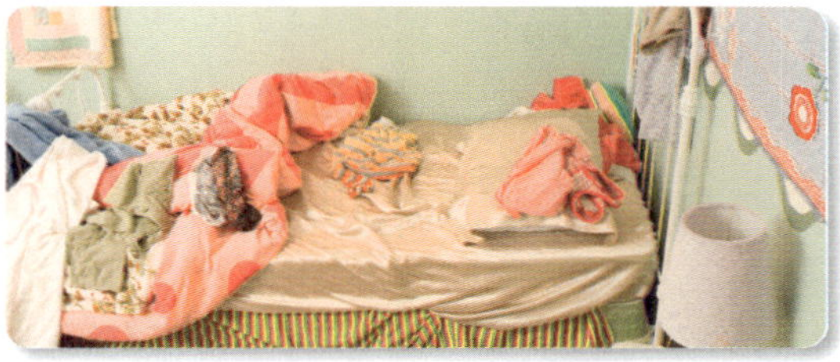

Liz won't clean her room on Sunday.

b. walk to school tomorrow (It's possible. / ✓)

We

c. see his friends on the weekend (It's possible. / X)

Miguel

d. do volunteer work on Friday (It's certain. / ✓)

They

DOWNLOADING

5 **Imagine that you have to move to another city. Look at the information in the box. Write three true sentences about you. Use *will*, *won't*, *might*, or *might not*.**

to miss my city | to have fun | to forget my friends | to make new friends | to like my new school | to start doing a new sport

Your turn!

Work with a partner. Share your sentences.

I might not miss my city.

Are you serious? I will miss my city. But I might not like my school.

LOADING

1 Listen and read the dialogues.

09 **a.**

b.

c.

2 Listen to the dialogues again and circle the correct alternatives.

10 **a.** In cartoon "A", it is **very possible / little possible** that Alison will move away next weekend.

b. In cartoon "B", it's **very possible / quite possible** that Anthony is moving away next weekend.

c. In cartoon "C", it's **little possible / very possible** that Ben will stay in the city.

Grammar feed

Degrees of possibility: *May*, *Could*, and *Might*

I **may move away** next weekend. → It is very possible that I will move away next weekend.
We **could move away** on Saturday, but there's still a lot to pack. → It is quite possible that we will move away next weekend.
I **might stay** in the city. → It's not very possible that I will stay in the city.

LEARNING STRATEGY

UPLOADING

3 **Complete the sentences with the most appropriate word: *may*, *could*, or *might*.**

a. They ______ ask me questions after my presentation, if we don't run out of time. (quite possible)

b. **A:** I want to visit Anne. Do you think she is at home today?

B: We ______ go there tomorrow, but let's check with Anne first. (quite possible)

c. It ______ rain this evening, do you think we need to change our plans? (not very possible)

d. I ______ come with you and meet our new neighbor. (not very possible)

e. If we don't hurry, we ______ be late for the party. (quite possible)

f. Nowadays people ______ travel all over Europe and not spend too much money. (very possible)

4 **Match the sentences and form dialogues.**

a. Where are John and Stella? They're late!

b. They're coming this week, but I don't know when.

c. When are you going to finish this report?

d. I'll call Mandy right now.

e. We could see a movie. What do you think?

( ) I wanted to finish it by tomorrow, but I am so tired! I guess I'll probably only finish it the day after tomorrow.

( ) She might be working now.

( ) They may be coming tomorrow.

( ) They might be stuck in traffic.

( ) I like that idea! But the weather forecast says it may rain today. Let's go by car.

DOWNLOADING

5 **Answer the questions below. Use *may* or *might* and the phrases from the box.**

~~to go to Holland~~ to be a little late to stay at home

a. What are your plans for next year?

I may go to Holland.

b. Are you going to arrive on time?

______

c. What are you going to do on the weekend?

______

iRead

1 Do you think teenagers often write to advice columns in magazines or websites? Would you ask for advice from these places? Why (not)?

2 Read the e-mail a 13-year-old girl wrote to an advice website and the reply she got.

— September 18, 2024 —

Dear Dr. Teens, I'm 13 years old and I'm having some trouble with my friends at school. I started high school (I live in Australia) at the beginning of the year, and made some great bonds with a large group of girls. It was all great until a month or so ago. Somehow, I became best friends with some of the boys in my class, too. I obviously tried to spend an equal amount of time with each group. When I hung out with the girls, the boys understood, but when I hung out with the boys, I could tell the girls weren't too happy. They're very nice people, so they didn't say anything, but they kind of exchanged looks. When I sat with my male friends, they would always try to interfere. The biggest problem is that I like one of the boys in the group (let's call him Ben), and one of my female friends said that she thinks I'm hanging out with the boys just because Ben is there. What can I do to make everyone happy? Do I have to choose one group over the other? Please help me.

— Clueless, 13

Dear Clueless,

You shouldn't have to choose one group over another. And it's okay if part of the reason you are hanging out with the group of boys is because you like Ben. Instead of trying to make everyone happy all the time, which is probably impossible, think about what makes you feel good. If you like spending time with that group of girls, then continue to do so, and make sure you let them know how much you enjoy hanging out with them. But you can certainly also spend time with the group of boys you've gotten friendly with. One strategy you might try is to set up an activity—maybe something music or sports-related—that both groups of friends would enjoy. That would allow the two groups to get to know each other and maybe even encourage the development of new friendships.

— Dr. Teens

3 Read the texts again and answer the questions.

see word pop-up page 150

a. Is the girl having trouble with her friends at school?

Yes, she is.

b. What do the girls do when she sits with the boys?

c. What pieces of advice does the counselor give the girl? Complete the list.

Not to choose

To think about

Try to set up

English for • *Ethics*

1 Is social media impacting real-life friendships? How? Exchange ideas with your teacher and classmates.

iThink

2 Read part of an article about the effects of technology on teen friendships.

Friendship has indeed changed in the digital age. But to what extent? Check out some important details and discover for yourself.

1. Over half, or 57%, of individuals have formed at least one new friendship online.
2. Out of the teenagers who have established friendships online, 64% state that they met through a social networking platform.
3. Some teenagers have encountered negative experiences on social media, as 68% report facing conflicts among friends on such platforms.
4. About 88% of individuals engage in conversations with their friends through text messaging on occasion, with 55% doing so daily.
5. Roughly a quarter, or 25%, have had disagreements with a friend because of an online incident or a text message.
6. Online gaming appears to hold significant importance in developing and sustaining friendships, with 78% of teens who play video games online saying that they feel more connected to their gaming friends.

READING STRATEGY

see word pop-up page 150

3 Read the text again and check (✓) the true statement(s).

a. More than 50% of teens have made a new friend online. ☐

b. Less than 90% of teens talk to their friends via text message every day. ☐

c. About 25% of teens have had a fight with friends because of something that happened online. ☐

d. Less than 78% of teens feel more connected to friends they play online games with. ☐

project

1 Look at the signs for one minute. Then close your books.

a. 

c. 

e. 

b. 

d. 

f. 

Work in pairs. Tell your partner about three of the signs. Use *must* or *must not*. Switch roles. Your partner will talk about the other three signs.

a. ____________________

b. ____________________

c. ____________________

d. ____________________

e. ____________________

f. ____________________

2 Work in pairs. Role-play a situation.

Student A: You are the principal of a middle school.
Student B: You are a new student.
You have to walk through the school. The principal has to tell the student what students *can*, *must*, and *must not do*. The student has to ask questions, such as *Can I leave an exam early?*
Take notes. Then create a poster about the school rules.

SCHOOL RULES

Self-Assessment

Circle the correct option to complete the sentences.

1. Friends **should / could** respect each other's new friends.
2. If he's always bothering you, you **shouldn't / should** take longer to respond to his texts and phone calls.
3. Students **must / may** take an entrance exam in the final year of elementary school to get into the middle school.
4. We **mustn't / might** not dress as stereotypes on Halloween.
5. **A:** Are you having dinner out tonight, Jane?
   B: I'd like to, but I can't. I **may / must** finish my geography paper.
6. I have an idea! We **could / can** play tennis tomorrow.
7. I promise I **will / should** text you every day, but maybe not all the time as we do now.
8. **A:** Peter is thirty minutes late.
   B: He **might / must** not come to the game then.
9. The children **may / might** go on a picnic on Thanksgiving Day. We are not sure yet, but it's very possible.
10. **A:** Are you going travel this weekend?
    B: I **might / can** go to the beach with my parents.

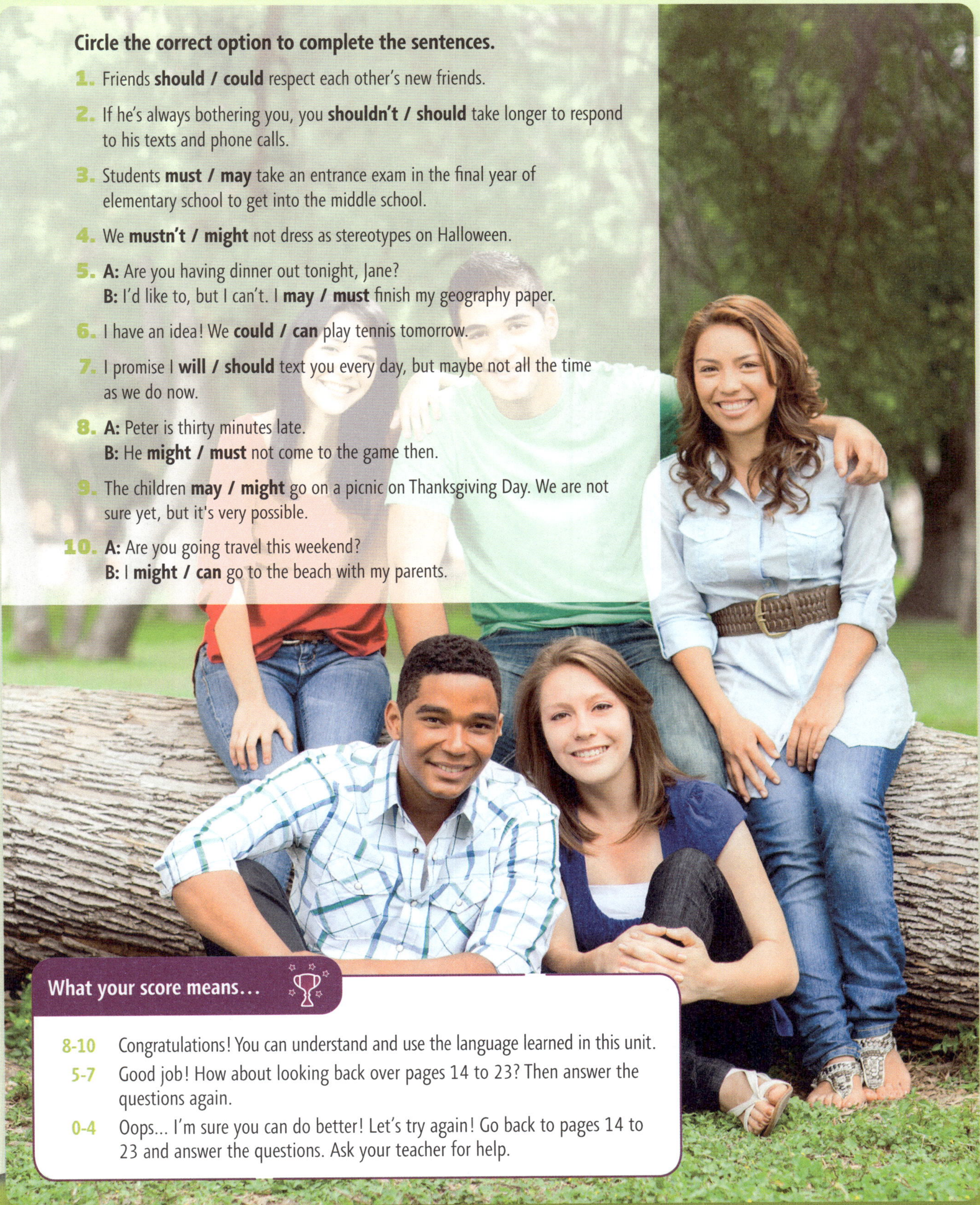

What your score means...

8-10 Congratulations! You can understand and use the language learned in this unit.
5-7 Good job! How about looking back over pages 14 to 23? Then answer the questions again.
0-4 Oops... I'm sure you can do better! Let's try again! Go back to pages 14 to 23 and answer the questions. Ask your teacher for help.

unit

2 I've cleaned my room.

» IN THIS UNIT YOU WILL

- talk about events in an indefinite time in the past
- discuss chores and responsibilities at home
- learn some indefinite time adverbs

START UP

Let's plug in! What can you see in the picture? Do you clean your own bedroom? Do you usually help keep the house clean? What do you do?

LOADING

1 **Lucas is going to hang out with some school friends in the afternoon. He calls Ian to see if he wants to go, too. Listen and read.**

12

Ian: Hello?

Lucas: Hi, Ian. It's Lucas.

Ian: Hi, Lucas. How are you doing?

Lucas: Fine! Listen… I'm going to that new ice cream parlor with some guys from my class this afternoon. Would you like to join us?

Ian: Sorry, I can't. On Friday afternoons I help my mom around the house.

Lucas: You must be kidding!

Ian: Why not? Don't tell me you don't help keep your house clean!

Lucas: Actually, I don't. What do you do?

Ian: Well, I don't do much from Monday to Thursday because my days are very busy. But I'm really happy to help on Fridays and Saturdays. On Fridays I clean my room and water the plants.

Lucas: OK, but can't you do them tomorrow?

Ian: No, Lucas. Tomorrow I'm going to do the washing.

Lucas: I see… And what time are you going to finish your chores today?

Ian: I'm not sure. I got home from school an hour ago. I've watered the plants, but I haven't cleaned my room.

Lucas: OK. I'll see you at the basketball game on Sunday then.

Ian: See you!

2 **Read the dialogue again. Then decide if the sentences are T (true) or F (false).**

a. Lucas wants Ian to go to a pizza place with him. T F

b. Ian doesn't like helping his mom around the house. T F

c. Ian has watered the plants, but he hasn't cleaned his room. T F

d. The boys will meet on Sunday. T F

3 **Listen again and repeat the dialogue.**

13

Grammar feed

Present Perfect: events at an indefinite time in the past

Affirmative	Ian **has watered** the plants.
Negative	He **hasn't cleaned** his room.

UPLOADING

4 **Jessica and Brian often help their mom around the house. This is their household chores checklist. Write sentences based on the information given. Use the list of irregular verbs on pages 144 and 145 to help you.**

	Jessica	Brian
to clean the kitchen		✔
to pick up the clutter	✔	
to do the laundry	✔	
to sweep the floor		✔

LEARNING STRATEGY

a. Jessica hasn't cleaned the kitchen, but she has picked up the clutter.

b. Jessica

c. Brian

d. Brian

5 **Use the prompts to write sentences in the Present Perfect. Write affirmative (✓) or negative (X) sentences. Use the list of irregular verbs on pages 144 and 145 to help you.**

a. We / make the beds (X)

We haven't made the beds.

b. They / wash the dishes (✔)

c. Louise / dust everywhere (X)

d. Dan / vacuum the carpets (✔)

DOWNLOADING

6 **Write two sentences about things you have done to help keep your house clean.**

a.

b.

Your turn!

Work with a partner. Share your sentences. Have you done anything similar? If so, what?

LOADING

1 **Two teens are talking about helping their parents. Listen and read.**

14

Hi! I'm Deborah. I don't mind helping my parents around the house. I have helped them for a long time. I usually plan meals and set the table. Yesterday I went shopping for food for the first time. It was a lot of fun. When I came back home, I helped my mom cook. Then I served dinner and cleaned the kitchen. My dad usually clears the table after dinner, but when he gets back home from work very late, I do it.

Hello! My name's Carlos. I don't like all the household chores my mom asks me to do, but there's something I really like to do – the laundry. I do the laundry twice a week. I started doing the laundry last year. At first, I just sorted the clothes into different colors. But then I started washing and drying them, too. My brother has helped me with this part sometimes, but now he doesn't usually help me with this. He folds the clothes after I finish drying them. We have a lot of fun doing the laundry together!

2 **Read the text again and complete the sentences.**

a. Yesterday Deborah ______________ .

b. She also ______________ , ______________ .

c. Carlos ______________ last year.

d. At first, he ______________ into different colors.

e. His brother ______________ him before.

Grammar feed

Simple Past vs. Present Perfect

Simple Past	**Present Perfect**
Definite time in the past Periods of time that have finished	Indefinite time in the past Periods of time that have not finished yet Repeated actions in the past
Yesterday Deborah **went** shopping for food. When she **came** back home, she **helped** her mom cook.	Debora **has helped** her parents for a long time now. Carlos' brother **has helped** him.

UPLOADING

3 **Complete the sentences with the verbs in parentheses. Use the Simple Past or the Present Perfect. Use the list of irregular verbs on pages 144 and 145 to help you.**

a. Kathy loves to cook. She [has cooked] all her mother's favorite recipes. Last week, she [prepared] roast chicken and mashed potatoes. (to cook / to prepare)

b. Ms. Spencer [ ] some of her pets. She [ ] time to feed all of them. (to feed / not to have)

c. The children [ ] the plants on Sunday, but they [ ] the garden. (to water / to tidy)

d. How many meals [ ] you [ ]? (to prepare)

4 **Rewrite the sentences to correct the underlined mistakes.**

a. How many beds have you made yesterday?

How many beds did you make yesterday?

b. I have gone shopping for food last Saturday.

c. I visited three different countries in my life.

d. My dad has folded our clothes and put them away yesterday evening.

DOWNLOADING

5 **Ask your classmate questions using the prompts in the chart.**

	Questions	My answers	My classmate's answers
a. Do the laundry / last weekend	Did you do the laundry last weekend?		
b. How many times / visit Argentina			
c. Clean your bedroom / yesterday			

Your turn!

Work with a partner. Take turns asking and answering the questions in Activity 5. Write your partner's answers in the chart.

LOADING

1 Listen and read these conversations.

15 **a.**

b.

c.

2 Read the conversations again. Underline the correct alternatives.

Conversation 1

Jane **has never baked/has baked** a cake.

Conversation 2

Ethan has watered the plants. He has **never planted/also planted plants**.

Conversation 3

It is one of the best movies **the girl/the girl's dad** has ever seen.

3 Listen again and repeat the dialogues.

16

Grammar feed

Present Perfect: *Yes/No* Questions

Have you ever **seen** *It*?		**Has** Jane ever **baked** a cake?
Affirmative	Yes, I **have**.	Yes, she **has**.
Negative	No, I **haven't**.	No, she **hasn't**.

UPLOADING

4 Match the two columns and form questions. Pay attention to the answers given.

a. **A:** Has Beatrice…
B: Not yet. But she has vacuumed her bedroom.

b. **A:** Have you ever…
B: Yes, we have cleaned it twice.

c. **A:** Has Lucy ever…
B: Yes, she painted it when she moved in.

d. **A:** Has Tyler…
B: No, he has never ironed any clothes.

e. **A:** Have the children…
B: Yes, they often do that. In fact, they help me a lot.

( ) ironed his clothes?
( ) vacuumed the living room?
( ) helped in the kitchen?
( ) painted the house?
( ) cleaned the garage?

5 Complete the questions. Then answer them using your own information.

a. Have you ever painted (to paint) your house?
_____, _____________________.

b. _____ you ever _____ (to eat) sushi?
_____, _____________________.

c. _____ you ever _____ (to bake) a cake?
_____, _____________________.

d. _____ you ever _____ (to iron) any clothes?
_____, _____________________.

DOWNLOADING

6 Work with a partner. Take turns asking and answering the questions in Activity 5. Take notes of your partner's answers in the chart.

Questions	Classmate's answers
a.	
b.	
c.	
d.	

Your turn!

Work with another pair. Share your partner's answers with them.

LOADING

1 **Phillip is getting ready for a two-week trip. He is going to work at a summer camp. His mother is calling him from work to see if he is ready. Listen and read.**

17

Phillip: Hello?

Mom: Hi, Phillip.

Phillip: Hi, Mom.

Mom: How's your packing going? Have you finished yet?

Phillip: Not yet, Mom.

Mom: But you need to finish tonight!

Phillip: I know. Right now I'm doing other chores. I've already organized my desk, but I haven't cleaned my bedroom yet.

Mom: Where's your sister? Can't she help you?

Phillip: I've already thought of that, Mom. I've asked her to make my bed and take out the trash.

Mom: Sounds good. Have you bought sunscreen yet?

Phillip: Yes, I have.

Mom: What else do you still need to do?

Phillip: Well, I've separated the clothes I want to take. But there are still some small things I need to think about, like sneakers.

Mom: I see. I'll help you finish packing tonight.

Phillip: Great, Mom. See you later then.

2 **Read the dialogue again. Then look at Phillip's list of chores. Cross out what he has already done.**

To do list
Buy sunscreen
Clean bedroom
Pack
Separate clothes

3 **Listen again and repeat the dialogue.**

18

Grammar feed

Present Perfect: *Already* and *Yet*

Affirmative	I've **already** organized my desk.
Negative	I haven't cleaned my bedroom **yet**.
Interrogative	Have you bought sunscreen **yet**?

UPLOADING

4 **Write sentences in the Present Perfect using the correct form of the verbs. Add *already* or *yet*. Pay attention to the symbols in parentheses.**

a. Phillip / to talk / to his mother (✓)

Phillip has already talked to his mother.

b. Phillip's sister / to take out / the trash (?)

______

c. The boys / to travel / to the summer camp (X)

______

d. Phillip / to buy / sunscreen. (✓)

______

5 **Phillip had to go to the supermarket to buy some things for his trip. He left his mother a note. Complete the note with the verbs in parentheses in the Present Perfect.**

Hi, Mom!

I had to go to the supermarket. I bought (to buy) the wrong sunscreen. It isn't SPF30. I ______ (to finish) packing yet, but I ______ already ______ (to separate) all my stuff on my bed. I ______ (to walk) Fido yet, but I'll do that as soon as I get back home. Just one thing: ______ you ______ (to ask) Sarah to help me with dinner? She said she won't do it because she ______ already ______ (to help) me a lot today.

Phillip

DOWNLOADING

6 **Imagine this is your *to do list*. Cross out the chores you have already done.**

Todolist

Clean your room	Walk the dog
Take out the trash	Wash the dishes
Make your bed	Do the laundry

Your turn!

Work with a partner. Imagine you are his/her parent. Ask questions to check the he/she has done the chores. Then switch roles.

Have you cleaned your room yet?

No, I haven't.

OR

Yes, I have.

iListen

1 **Zac is talking to his aunt about getting some money from doing chores. Listen to their conversation and check (✓) the sentences that are true.**

19

a. Zac's aunt is tired. ☐

b. Zac's aunt is planning a birthday party. ☐

c. Zac can go to her house the following afternoon. ☐

d. Zac's aunt is going to pay him $10 for all the chores. ☐

e. There aren't many chores for Zac to do. ☐

iWrite

2 **What chores would you like to do to get some extra money? How much would you charge for each chore? Write your ideas in the chart.**

Activities	How much would you charge?

iSpeak

3 **Work with a partner. Share your ideas from Activity 2.**

I've already walked dogs. I can do it for $2 an hour. What about you?

I've never wrapped gifts. I can do it for $0.50 for each gift. .

English for • *Culture*

1 **Do you help your family by doing chores? What do you usually do? Exchange ideas with your teacher and classmates.**

iThink

2 **Read some quotes about gender equality.**

READING STRATEGY

1

"Raise boys and girls with the same values: respect, empathy, and equality."

Anonymous

2

"Gender equality is not just a women's issue, it's a human issue."

Anonymous

3

"Education is the great equalizer, let's make it accessible to all."

Anonymous

see word pop-up page 154

3 **Read and write write 1, 2, or 3.**

project

What quote…

- [ ] says that Education can help in gender equality?
- [ ] talks about teaching the same values to boys and girls?
- [ ] says that gender equality is everyone's issue?

rePlay

1 Play *Two Truths and a Lie.*

1. Work in groups of five.
2. On a piece of paper, write three sentences about yourself; two sentences should be true and one should be false. Use the Present Perfect.
3. Read your three sentences to your group. Your group must guess which sentence is false.
4. The student who guesses correctly gets a point. The student with the most points is the winner.

I have already baked a some bread!

2 Play *Tic-Tac-Toe.*

1. Work with a partner. Choose X or O.
2. To win a square, come up with a sentence (affirmative, negative, or interrogative) using the verb in the Present Perfect.
3. If the sentence is correct, you can mark the square. Then it's your partner's turn to try.
4. The winner is the first person to mark three squares in a row.

TO WATER	TO CLEAN	TO VACUUM
TO BAKE	TO SWEEP	TO TIDY
TO PREPARE	TO COOK	TO SET

3 Play *Say yes!*

1. Work with a partner. You have five minutes to ask your partner some questions.
2. Every time your partner answers "Yes, I have.", you get one point.
3. The winner is the person with the most points.

Have you ever washed clothes?

Yes, I have.

Self-Assessment

Circle the correct option to complete the sentences.

a. I**'ve watered/watered** the plants, but I haven't cleaned my room.

b. Yesterday Deborah **went/has gone** shopping for food.

c. Brian **didn't take/hasn't taken** out the trash yet.

d. **A:** Have you finished cleaning the garage **yet/already**?
B: Not yet. But I'll finish it in an hour.

e. **A:** Have you ever seen *The Hobbit*?
B: No, **ever/never.**

f. **A: Did you cook/Have you cooked** Italian food on Sunday?
B: Yes, I did. And everybody liked it!

g. I've **yet/already** organized my desk.

h. Has Diana **yet/ever** ironed her clothes?

i. When she **came/has come** back home, she helped her mom cook.

j. **Did Brian finish/Has Brian finished** packing yet?

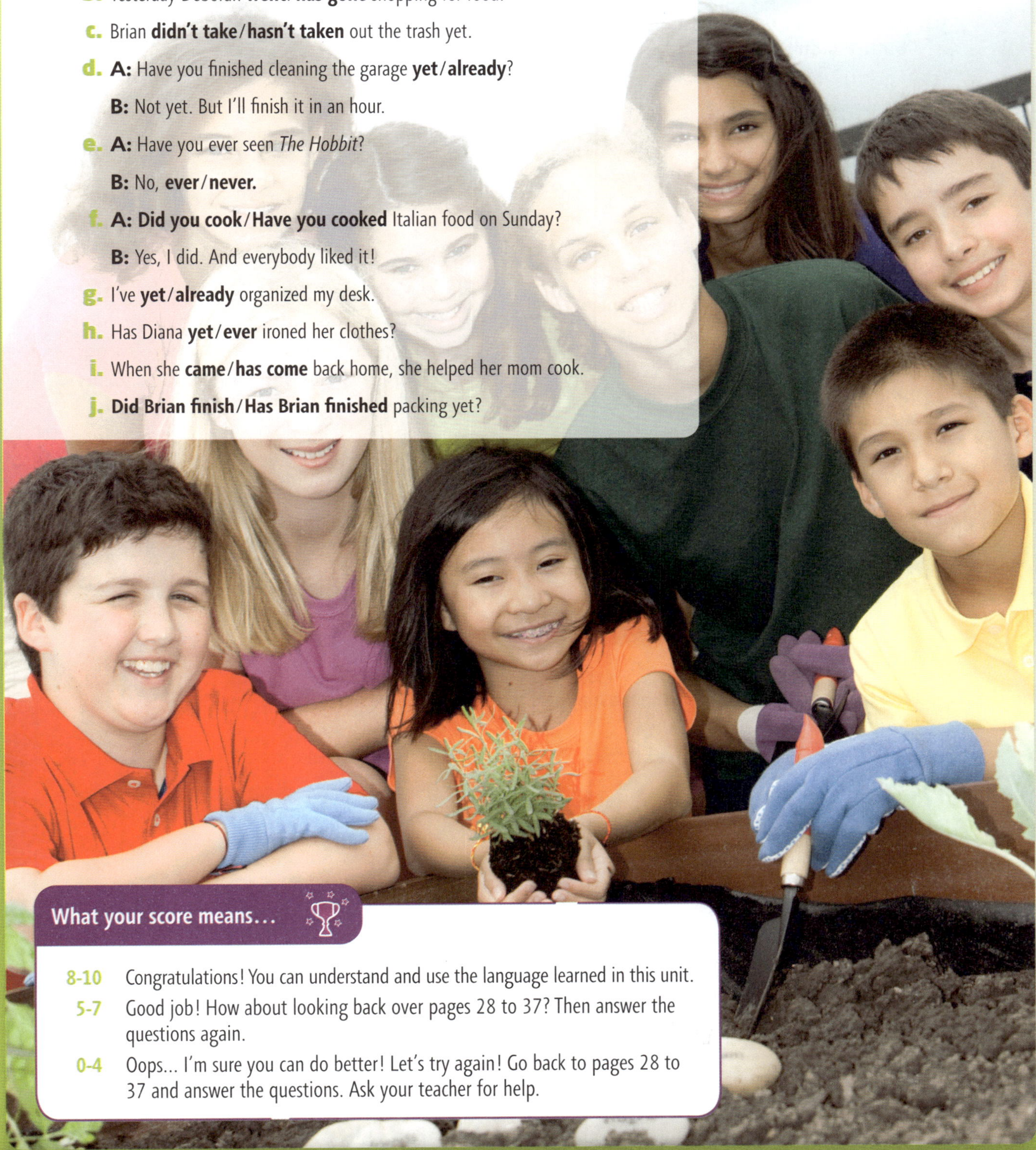

What your score means...

8-10 Congratulations! You can understand and use the language learned in this unit.

5-7 Good job! How about looking back over pages 28 to 37? Then answer the questions again.

0-4 Oops... I'm sure you can do better! Let's try again! Go back to pages 28 to 37 and answer the questions. Ask your teacher for help.

Rewind 1 Units 1 - 2

1 Read the messages below. Then complete the answers their friends gave them.

a. "Today I was in class doing a test and I was really hungry. I asked my teacher, Mr. Jones, if I could go outside and buy something to eat, but he didn't let me! Was he right?"

Of course he was right! You can't ______________________

b. "My friend Rob forgot his homework activity at home and then he just stole mine! Can you believe it? What should I do? Do you have any suggestions?"

You should ______________________

c. "Today I went to my cousin's place and he wasn't there. I left him a message to call me soon. I want to invite him to my birthday party! Do you think he will call me?"

Relax! I'm sure he will ______________________

d. "My friends and I want to go out on Saturday afternoon, but we can't make up our minds on where to go. Do you have any suggestions for us?

Well, you could go ______________________

2 Read the cartoon and check (✓) the most appropriate answers.

"Because my students have to be reminded constantly."

a. *Have to* is used in the sentence to express...
- [ ] probability/possibility.
- [ ] obligation/necessity.

b. We can infer that the teacher is wearing that T-shirt because she...
- [ ] really wants to help her students.
- [ ] wants to avoid asking students to think.

c. The cartoon can be considered...
- [ ] quite offensive.
- [ ] really funny.

3 Complete these e-mails with the verbs in parentheses in the Simple Past or the Present Perfect.

a. **New comment**

I think I ________ really ________ (to hurt) several people's feelings. Yesterday I ________ (to say) something insensitive to Friend A about Friend B and Friend C, and I don't think any of them will like me now. I feel really guilty. What should I do?

– Elizabeth.

Send

b. **New comment**

School's starting soon. Last year I ________ (to bully) this boy (I'm a girl). I ________ (to attack) him even though he's stronger because I ________ (to know) he wouldn't hit a girl. I ________ (to insult) him. I ________ (to humiliate) him every chance I got. I want to start over. I want to apologize, but I don't know how. I feel awful for doing this. He doesn't trust me. How do I show him I ________ (to change)?

– Jess

Send

4 Use the prompts below to write true sentences about you. Use *already* or *yet*.

a. to organize my desk

I have already organized my desk. OR I haven't organized my desk yet.

b. to have lunch

c. to go to Chile

d. to do my homework

5 Now answer these questions. Give short answers.

a. Have you cleaned your room yet?

b. Have you ever cleaned the garage?

c. Has your best friend ever ironed her/his clothes?

d. Has any member of your family ever painted their house?

unit

3 How does social media affect our lives?

» IN THIS UNIT YOU WILL

- talk about actions that happened in the past, but are close to the present
- use time expressions to refer to the beginning or duration of an action
- understand the difference between the Simple Present and the Present Perfect
- learn how to use the adverbs *too* and *enough*

START UP

Let's plug in! What can you see in the picture? Are you addicted to social media? What are the benefits of using social media? Share your ideas with your teacher and classmates.

LOADING

1 **Jack is reading an online article. Read and listen to his conversation with his wife Cammie.**

20

Did you know...?

- More people own a mobile device than a toothbrush.
- Facebook is the largest country on earth.
- X, formerly Twitter is most popular among users aged 25-34.
- The most popular hashtags for Instagram posts are #love, #instagood, #me, #cute, and #follow.
- There are more than one billion users on YouTube, which is nearly one-third of all internet users.

Cammie: Are you reading today's news, Jack?
Jack: No, I've already read it. I've just started reading an impressive article!
Cammie: What's it about?
Jack: It's about how social media is changing the world.
Cammie: Hmm… it must be interesting.
Jack: It really is. Did you know that more people own a mobile device than a toothbrush?
Cammie: That's not true!
Jack: That's what the article says. And you know what? Grandparents are the fastest growing users.
Cammie: Really? I knew our parents' habits had changed since they got access to the Internet, but I didn't know it was that much.

2 **Read the dialogue again. Then underline the sentence that expresses an action that happened in the past, but is very close to the present.**

Grammar feed

Present Perfect: *Just*

Jack **has just started** reading an impressive online article.

A: Come here and help me set the table, honey!

B: Hold on, Mom! **I've just arrived**. I need to wash my hands first.

UPLOADING

3 **Complete the sentences with the verbs in parentheses in the Present Perfect and find out what some people have done. Use *just*.**

a. We have just watched his new video on YouTube. (to watch)

b. My grandpa ________ a new cell phone. (to buy)

c. He ________ me a message on Facebook. (to send)

d. The journalists ________ about the catastrophe. (to tweet)

e. Martha ________ me. She has already left school. (to text)

f. Bert ________ a free music streaming app. (to download)

4 **Answer the questions using *just*.**

a. Have you bought that media-streaming player yet?

Yes, I've just bought it.

b. Have you found the public Wi-Fi network yet?

____

c. Have you recorded that video with your cell phone yet?

____

d. Have you uploaded all the videos yet?

____

DOWNLOADING

5 **Look at the picture below for 30 seconds. Then close your books. Work in pairs. Talk about what these people have just done.**

LOADING

1 **Read and listen to these testimonials about social media. Do you agree with any of them? Which one? Why? Explain.**

21

I made a Facebook profile when I was 13 because it was cool, so I have had it for four years now. It's strange to be on Facebook. It can be annoying sometimes. But not having a Facebook profile can be even more annoying. People come to you and say "Everybody is on Facebook, why aren't you?" I don't feel comfortable enough to decline a friend request. But sometimes I don't want to talk to that person, you know? To me, Facebook is the jumping-off point for many people to try to find you online.

Elizabeth Mackay

Instagram is the most used social media application for my age group. Although most people are on Facebook, we actually post stuff on Instagram. I created my account a year ago. I have posted 250 photos since then and have gotten thousands of likes. To me, the content on Instagram is usually of higher quality. People take time to edit their photos and make them look the best they can. I also like the fact that there are no links on Instagram, so I am not constantly spammed by the same ad.

Matthew Hugs

2 **Read the testimonials again and write *E* for Elizabeth or *M* for Matthew.**

a. This person doesn't like to be spammed by the same ad. ____

b. This person has gotten thousands of likes on her/his photos. ____

c. This person doesn't feel comfortable declining a friend request. ____

Grammar feed

Present Perfect: *Since* and *For*

I **have posted** 250 photos **since** I created the account.	I **have had** a Facebook profile **for** four years now.
↓ beginning of the period	↓ duration of the period

UPLOADING

3 **Kathryn is addicted to technology. Look at some events in her life and complete the sentences. Use *since* or *for*.**

a. Kathryn [has used] Facebook and Instagram [since 2014 / for... years].

b. She [ ] an iPad and a cell phone [ ].

c. She [ ] music and [ ] YouTube videos [ ].

d. She [ ] more than 100 videos with her cell phone [ ].

e. She [ ] 28 online books [ ].

DOWNLOADING

4 **How do you use social media? Write three sentences similar to the ones in Activity 3.**

[ ]

[ ]

[ ]

[ ]

Your turn!

Work with a partner. Compare your sentences.

I have watched YouTube videos for a few months.

I have recorded a few videos with my cell phone since my birthday.

LOADING

1 **Look at the bar chart below. Has the number of social media users increased continuously since 2010? Read the text and check your answer.**

Number of social media users worldwide from 2010 to 2021 (in billions)

This chart shows the number of social media users worldwide from 2010 to 2016 and projections up to 2021. In 2019, it is estimated that there will be around 2.77 billion social media users around the globe, up from 2.46 billion in 2017.

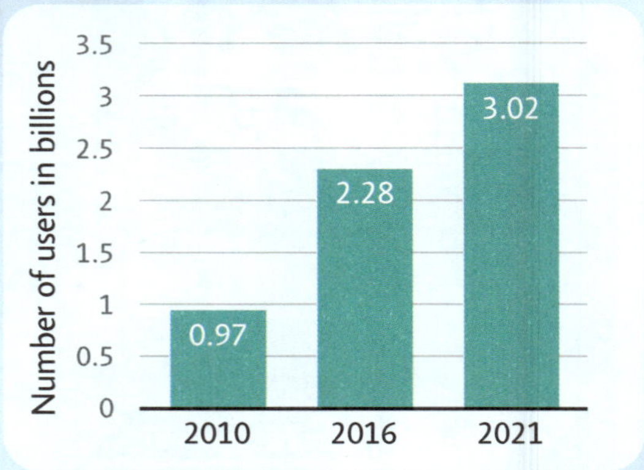

Social media users

Social network penetration worldwide is ever-increasing. In 2017, 71 percent of Internet users were social network users and these figures are expected to grow. Social networking is one of the most popular online activities with high user engagement rates and expanding mobile possibilities. North America ranks first among regions where social media is highly popular, with a social media penetration rate of 66 percent. In 2016, more than 81 percent of the population had a social media profile. As of the second quarter of 2016, U.S. users spent more than 215 weekly minutes on social media via smartphones, 61 weekly minutes via PCs, and 47 minutes per week on social networks via tablet devices.

The increased worldwide usage of smartphones and mobile devices has opened up the possibilities of mobile social networks, with increased features such as location-based services like Foursquare or Google Now. Most social networks are also available as mobile social apps, whereas some networks have been optimized for mobile internet browsing, enabling users to comfortably access visual blogging sites such as Tumblr or Pinterest via tablet.

see word pop-up page 158

2 **Read the text again. Write T (true) or F (false).**

a. The number of social media users may increase from 2017 to 2019. ☐

b. Social media is very popular, especially in North America. ☐

c. In 2016, U.S. users spent more time per week on social media via PC than on any other device. ☐

Grammar feed

Simple Present vs. Present Perfect

Facts

This chart **shows** the number of social media users worldwide. North America **ranks** first among regions where social media is highly popular.

Routine activities

She checks her Facebook account twice a day.

Duration of facts/events

The number of social media users worldwide **has increased** since 2010.

HOW LONG

People **have stayed** in touch with social networks for a few years.

UPLOADING

3 **Circle the correct answers.**

a. Today I **have** / **have had** a few social media profiles.
b. How long **are you** / **have you been** on Facebook?
c. How often **do you text** / **have you texted** your friends?
d. Lynn **reads** / **has read** a lot of online books since she got her e-Reader.
e. My parents **use** / **have used** Pinterest for a few months.

4 **Read two other paragraphs of the text in Activity 1 and complete the sentences with the verbs in parentheses. Use the Simple Present or the Present Perfect.**

With over 1.86 billion monthly active users, the social network Facebook is currently the market leader in terms of reach and scope. The site has been shaping the social media landscape since its launch and ______ (to be) an important factor in discussions about users' privacy and differentiating between one's private and public online self.

Social networks not only ______ (to enable) users to communicate beyond local or social boundaries, but also ______ (to offer) possibilities to share user-generated content like photos and videos and features such as social games. Social advertising and social gaming are two major points of revenue for social networks.

DOWNLOADING

5 **Work with a partner. Read the information about Mika. Then take turns asking and answering questions about her life.**

- Study at Osaka International School / 2 years
- Use cell phone as a learning tool / last year
- Have a pet bird / six months
- Stop reading print books / she got an e-Reader

Where does Mika study?

She studies at Osaka International School.

How long has she used her cell phone as a learning tool?

She has used it as a learning tool since last year.

LOADING

1 **Gloria is texting her son Juan. Read their conversation.**

LEARNING STRATEGY

2 **Read their conversation again and check (✓) the true sentence(s).**

a. Juan usually replies to all his mother's messages. ☐

b. A new phone costs a lot of money. ☐

c. He wouldn't like to get a new cell phone. ☐

d. Juan is sad that his mom was joking. ☐

Grammar feed

Too* vs. *Enough

A new phone is **too** expensive anyway.	Juan doens't reply fast **enough** when his mom asks for his help.
too + adjective	adjective + enough

UPLOADING

3 **Unscramble the words and complete these sentences.**

a. I left the tea to cool because…
drink / to / hot / too / was / it

… it was too hot to drink.

b. He / strong / enough / wasn't

… to lift those heavy boxes.

c. It / too / isn't / difficult

… for a small child to do.

d. We didn't buy that cell phone model because…
expensive / was / too / it

e. She / enough / old / isn't

… to start driving.

4 **Complete these sentences of cell phone reviews. Use *too* or *enough*.**

a. If the latest phones are ______ expensive, consider an older-generation phone. For example, we still think that phones launched one or two years ago are better value than many new generation phones. There is a great phone which is now available for under $400 SIM-free.

b. Additionally, try asking your friends to take a picture of a colorful object, like a trinket box, that is small ______ for you to carry. Even if you're not intending to purchase that specific model, similar smartphones from the same maker might have the same sensors and processing software, leading to comparable outcomes.

DOWNLOADING

5 **Write two sentences that describe you. Use *too* and *enough*.**

Work in small groups. Share your sentences. Are they similar?

iRead

1 **Do you follow any bloggers? Who? Do you admire him/her? Why? Exchange ideas with your teacher and classmates.**

iThink

2 **Read about two young bloggers that have captivated the minds of readers on the Internet.**

Teen Dream: Being a Top Blogger Under 18

It's the digital age, baby. Kids are learning how to use technology at younger and younger ages, and, in turn, are starting their blogging careers before they can vote. Here are two inspiring teen bloggers who started at a young age.

Willie, 18

At the age of 18, Willie Greene was the founder and editor-in-chief of one of the fastest growing fashion blogs which was founded in 2009. His blog with an eclectic mix of art, music, fashion, and culture has garnered over five million views.

Tavi, 17

At the age of 11, this wonderful tween started a blog about fashion that landed her on the covers of famous magazines.

As a young style maven, Tavi Gevinson partnered with the London based Borders & Frontiers to design and sell her own T-shirt line and was the inspiration behind a famous American brand of clothing and accessories. Today, she has her own web magazine.

see word pop-up page 158

3 **Read the sentences and check (✓) the right box.**

a. Who has produced a blog about different topics, including music?

☐ Willie ☐ Tavi

b. Who started a blog at the age of 11?

☐ Willie ☐ Tavi

c. Who has a web magazine now?

☐ Willie ☐ Tavi

4 **Answer the questions.**

a. Which of these two bloggers would you follow? Why?

b. In your opinion, why do people follow bloggers?

English for • *Culture*

1 **In your opinion, why are YouTube stars so popular? Exchange ideas with your teacher and classmates. Then read the following online news article and check your guesses.**

Why are YouTube stars so popular?

Stuart Dredge
@stuartdredge
Wednesday 3 February
2016.12.59 GMT

With millions of subscribers, top YouTubers such as Zoella have huge, passionate audiences. Here's a handy guide to help you understand their popularity.

1 British vlogger Zoella has just reached the milestone of 10m subscribers to her main YouTube channel, but she has a long way to go to catch its most popular creator PewDiePie, who is about to pass 42m.

2 They're just two of the most prominent YouTube stars. In October 2015, online-video tracking firm Tubular Labs reported that there were more than 17,000 YouTube channels with more than 100,000 subscribers, and nearly 1,500 with more than 1m.

3 How have these YouTubers become so popular? It is hard for people outside their main viewing demographic to understand: smartphone-toting "millennials" who spend as much time (if not more) watching short-form video online as they do traditional TV shows.

4 YouTubers were judged to be more engaging, extraordinary, and relatable than mainstream stars, who were rated as being smarter and more reliable.

5 Looking at survey comments and feedback, teens enjoy an intimate and authentic experience with YouTube celebrities, who aren't subject to image strategies carefully orchestrated by public relations pros.

6 That's one of the key things to understand about the popularity of YouTubers – for their fans, the contrast with stars from the world of music, movies, and television has been a big factor in their rise.

7 Their very ordinariness – their relatability – is what makes them so appealing.

2 **Read these sentences and decide which paragraph they can go at the end of. Write the number of the paragraph.**

READING STRATEGY

project

☐ Teens also say they appreciate YouTube stars' more candid sense of humor, lack of filter, and risk-taking spirit, behaviors often curbed by Hollywood handlers.

☐ The "girl or boy next door" who is "just like us" is not an unusual trope in the entertainment world, but on YouTube, it's heightened.

rePlay

1 **Work with a partner. Combine the words to write sentences. You can use the same word more than once. How many sentences can you write in two minutes?**

you have we like has test the mall to she he for I play
games hasn't studied live in Italy Spain to been have English

I play games.

2 **Write the time expressions in the correct column. You have one minute.**

3 hours two months yesterday January 3rd 8:30 a.m. a few minutes
a few hours 2010 a long time dinner time last year four years

Since	For
last year	3 hours

Self-Assessment

Circle the correct option to complete the sentences.

a. I **have just started** / **started** reading an impressive article.

b. More people **have owned** / **own** a mobile device than a toothbrush nowadays.

c. Our parents' habits have changed **since** / **for** they got access to the Internet.

d. I **have just arrived** / **arrive**, Mom! I'll wash my hands and help you.

e. **A:** Have you bought a media-streaming player yet?
B: Yes, I **bought** / **have just bought** one.

f. I have had a Facebook profile **for** / **since** four years now.

g. The number of social media users worldwide **has increased** / **increases** since 2010.

h. How long **you have** / **have you had** your bike?

i. The coffee was **too hot** / **hot enough** to drink. I burned my mouth!

j. Mariana isn't **old enough** / **too old** to start driving. She is only 15.

What your score means...

8-10 Congratulations! You can understand and use the language learned in this unit.

5-7 Good job! How about looking back over pages 44 to 53? Then answer the questions again.

0-4 Oops... I'm sure you can do better! Let's try again! Go back to pages 44 to 53 and answer the questions. Ask your teacher for help.

unit 4

Great things about growing old.

» IN THIS UNIT YOU WILL

- talk about actions that have not finished yet
- learn how to use Reflexive Pronouns
- express how people do things
- understand the differences between some intensifiers

START UP

Let's plug in! What can you see in the picture? Do the people in the photo represent most of the older people you know? If so, how? Explain.

LOADING

1 **Sarah Johnson is a journalist. She is writing an article about the role of older people in society. Listen and read two testimonials from her interview.**

22

We have lived through situations you cannot even imagine. We have a lot of experience and skills, and we have different expectations these days. I don't want to end up in a care home, worrying about the usual things such as health, mortality, etc. I want to get up early every day, make my own coffee, and go for a walk with a few friends. I walk from five to six kilometers every morning. I have walked twenty seven kilometers this week. It's important to do exercise regularly. It makes me happy, it brings me lots of health benefits, and it gives me energy to work. Being an event planner is demanding. I have to travel regularly to attend the events I organize.

I have created a new life for myself and I have made it meaningful. I have a reason to get up in the morning. I want to make a difference in the world, so I've started doing volunteer work. I teach other seniors. I've planned five lessons so far. This way, I help them understand that their experience can contribute in different ways. They see how they can use their abilities to make an important impact. So why should I feel useless? I have an active social life, too. I talk with my grandchildren and their friends a lot. They come here once a month for a barbecue. I really believe that relaxing and spending time with them has a positive effect on my health.

2 **Read the texts again and check (✓) the true sentence.**

a. Both Alexia and Franklin have an active social life. ☐

b. Alexia has an active social life, but Franklin doesn't. ☐

c. Alexia has walked over 20 kilometers this week. ☐

d. Franklin volunteers at an animal shelter. ☐

Grammar feed

Present Perfect

Actions/events at an indefinite time in the past: we do not know when they happened

We **have lived** through situations you cannot even imagine.

I **have created** a new life for myself.

Actions/events in periods of time that have not finished yet

I **have walked** twenty seven kilometers **this week**.

I**'ve planned** five lessons **so far**.

UPLOADING

3 **Complete the sentences with the verbs in the Present Perfect. Then match the sentences with the pictures.**

a. Laura [has missed] two swimming classes this week. She's working on a conference outside the city. (to miss)

b. Dan ______ a medal in the judo competition. (to win)

c. Adam and his friends ______ to the movies. They aren't back yet. (to go)

d. I ______ my volunteer work. Now I'm surfing the net. (to do)

e. How many times ______ you ______ for your dance presentation this month? (to practice)

f. We ______ abroad twice this year. (to travel)

4 **Complete the questions with the Present Perfect form of the verbs in parentheses.**

a. How many classes [have] you [missed] this year? (to miss)

b. How many books ______ you ______ this month? (to read)

c. How many times ______ your best friend ______ to your house this week? (to go)

d. How many photos ______ you ______ online over the last few months? (to post)

DOWNLOADING

5 **Work with a partner. Take turns asking and answering the questions in Activity 4. Are your answers similar or different?**

How many classes have you missed this year?

I've missed one class. How about you? How many classes have you missed this year?

LOADING

1 **Naomi was surprised when she arrived at her house and saw her grandma playing the piano. Listen and read their conversation.**

23

Naomi: Hi, Granny! What are you doing?

Granny: Oh, hi, Naomi! I'm teaching myself to play the piano.

Naomi: I see... Don't you think you already play a lot of instruments?

Granny: I do, dear. But I love music! And I really like learning new things.

Naomi: I know. Can you stop playing it when my classmates get here, please? We're going to rehearse for the school drama presentation.

Granny: Sure! Can I join you?

Naomi: Well, if you think you'll enjoy yourself...

Granny: Of course I will!

2 **Read the dialogue again. Decide if the sentences are true (T) or false (F).**

a. Naomi's grandma doesn't know how to play any musical instruments. T F

b. Naomi is teaching her grandma how to play the piano. T F

c. Naomi and her classmates are going to rehearse for the school drama presentation. T F

3 **Rewrite the statements that are false in Activity 2 and correct them.**

______

______

______

______

Study this

Reflexive Pronouns

I	→	myself
You	→	yourself
He	→	himself
She	→	herself
It	→	itself
You	→	yourselves
We	→	ourselves
They	→	themselves

4 **Listen again and repeat the dialogue.**

24

UPLOADING

5 **Naomi threw a party at her house after her school drama presentation. Read the sentences, complete them with the Reflexive Pronouns, and guess what happened during the party.**

a. 

John was slicing some cheese when he cut himself.

b. 

Check it out, guys! I made the cake ______.

c. 

We really enjoyed ______. We danced a lot!

d. 

A: Did you hurt ______?

B: No, I'm OK. Thanks!

6 **Unscramble the words and form sentences.**

a. accident / blame / for / shouldn't / the / you / yourself

You shouldn't blame yourself for the accident.

b. I / hair / myself / my / cut

______

c. herself / introduced / never / She

______

d. enjoyed / have / much / themselves / They / very

______

DOWNLOADING

7 **Answer the questions with your personal information.**

	My answers	My partner's answers
When was the last time you hurt yourself?		
Do you sometimes talk to yourself?		
How often do you look at yourself in the mirror?		

Your turn!

Now work with a partner. Ask him/her the questions and take notes. Then report your partner's answers to the class.

Beatriz hurt herself when she fell off her bike last year.

LOADING

1 These are Alexia's friends, the ones who walk with her every morning. Read the sentences and number the pictures.

a. Diana swims well. When she was 64, she swam from Cuba to Florida. The journey was 110 miles long and took her 53 hours straight.

b. William is 92 years old and still runs fast. He has just come back from Honolulu. He ran a marathon there! He finished the race in less than eight hours.

c. Angelina plays the flute beautifully. She has taken part in many concerts since she started playing.

d. Anthony speaks four languages. He speaks all of them well, but German is the one he speaks perfectly.

2 Listen and repeat the sentences.

25

Grammar feed

Adverbs of Manner

Diana **swims** well.
William **runs** fast.
→ Verb + Adverb

Angelina **plays** the flute beautifully.
Anthony **speaks** German perfectly.
→ Verb + Object + Adverb

Study this

Adjectives	→	Adverbs
bad	→	badly
beautiful	→	beautifully
perfect	→	perfectly
quiet	→	quietly
fast	→	fast
good	→	well
hard	→	hard

UPLOADING

3 **Choose the most suitable word to complete the sentences.**

a. It is difficult to understand my teacher when he talks too ________.

☐ quickly ☐ slowly

b. We always study ________ for the big tests.

☐ hard ☐ hardly

c. She did really ________ in her tennis match last week.

☐ good ☐ well

d. I don't want to move. I'm sitting ________.

☐ normally ☐ comfortably

e. This is a very important question. Please think about it ________.

☐ carefully ☐ careful

4 **Read an extract about senior living communities and underline the adverbs of manner. Then complete the chart with the verb and the adverbs related to it.**

Senior living communities provide peace of mind for everyone, offering older adults the opportunity to maintain an active social life that helps them physically, spiritually, and mentally. At the same time, they give family and friends the assurance that their loved ones have a safe and joyful environment to reside in.

Verb	Adverb

DOWNLOADING

5 **Write an ending for each sentence. Use adverbs. In groups of three, read your sentences and decide on the best ones.**

a. John Green is my favorite novelist. I think he writes ________.

b. I don't think we played ________.

c. My dad drives ________ and that makes me nervous.

LOADING

1 **Kelly Rotas likes posting about people that accomplished amazing things after they turned 50. Read what she has posted recently.**

Kelly Rotas

♡325 Q67

@kellyrotas
Artist Grandma Moses started painting at age 78 after she was diagnosed with arthritis. Now her art is at MOMA. She paints really well!

3:25 P.M. - Aug 12, 2017

Kelly Rotas

♡413 Q70

@kellyrotas
Tightrope walker William Ivy Baldwin walked across a canyon on his 82nd birthday. He's quite brave!

1:15 P.M. - Aug 23, 2017

2 **Read the posts again and identify the two words Kelly uses to intensify adverbs and adjectives.**

____

____

____

Study this

LEARNING STRATEGY

***Really*, *Very*, and *Quite* + adjectives or adverbs**

The water is **really** cold.
The boys did **very** well in the test.
She is **quite** talented.

UPLOADING

3 **Listen to four conversations. Who/What are they talking about? What intensifiers + adjectives or adverbs do they use?**

26

a.	Johnny's new car	really expensive and fast
b.		
c.		
d.		

4 **Rewrite the sentences using the words in parentheses in the correct position.**

a. The weather is beautiful today. (really)

The weather is really beautiful today.

b. It was a good party, wasn't it? (very)

c. My boss is old. (quite)

d. I think history is a hard subject. (very)

e. John's car is great, but it is slow. (quite)

DOWNLOADING

5 **Work with a partner. Have conversations similar to the one below.**

Is your neighborhood nice?

Well, there are some parts that are old. But there are really nice places to go to, so I like my neighborhood a lot.

Your turn!

Ask your partner if:

- his/her apartment/house is big
- his/her neighborhood is old

iRead

1 **Do you remember anything about Grandma Moses? What do you remember?**

2 **Read part of Grandma Moses' biography and find out further information about her.**

LEARNING STRATEGY

Grandma Moses

Painter (1860–1961)

Anna Mary Robertson, who is also known as "Grandma Moses," gained fame for her nostalgic artworks portraying life in rural America.

Life as a Farmer, Wife, and Mother

Anna Mary Robertson was born on September 7, 1860, in Greenwich, New York. She was more popularly known as Grandma Moses, one of the most renowned folk artists of the twentieth century. Her parents had a farm where she grew up with nine other siblings. At the age of 12, Moses left home and began working on a farm nearby.

In 1887, she got married to Thomas Moses, and they settled in the Shenandoah Valley of Virginia. Together, they managed a farm and raised five children (they also lost five infants).

In 1905, Moses returned to New York with her family, where she and her husband ran a farm in Eagle Bridge. Moses began experimenting with painting in 1918, creating her first work on a fireboard in her home. Although she painted occasionally, she didn't fully commit to her art until later in life. After her husband died in 1927, Moses sought ways to keep herself occupied during her grief.

Artist Grandma Moses lived the rural, agricultural life depicted in her paintings for many years before fully dedicating herself to art in her seventies. In 1938, a collector discovered her artwork, and despite being self-taught, Moses gained fame for her portrayals of country life. She passed away in 1961 at the age of 101.

3 **Check the correct answers.**

a. In 1887, she got married to Thomas Moses, and they settled in the Shenandoah Valley of Virginia. *Settle* probably means:

- [ ] go to live somewhere permanently
- [ ] leave your house

b. Moses returned to New York with her family, where she and her husband ran a farm in Eagle Bridge. *Ran*, past tense of *run*, probably means:

- [ ] buy
- [ ] control, organize

see word pop-up page 162

4 **Read the text again and complete the sentences.**

a. An art collector discovered her work in 1938.

b. She didn't paint before ________.

c. She got married in ________.

d. She created her first work ________.

1 What simple activities could older people do in order to improve their health? Did you know that walking a dog is an effective way of keeping the body and mind healthy in later life? Do you agree with this? Why? Exchange ideas with your teacher and classmates.

iThink

2 Read the text and find out what a newspaper journalist says about this.

READING STRATEGY

Dogs can help older people increase physical activity

A recent study suggests that elderly individuals should receive dogs as a treatment option to increase their outdoor physical activity. According to researchers from the University of Cambridge and the University of East Anglia (UEA), having a dog or walking one is a highly effective method for combating the typical decrease in activity that comes with aging.

The report also encouraged older adults to venture outside even in unpleasant weather, as doing so can enhance their mood and overall health.

Over 3000 elderlies participating in the study were surveyed about dog ownership and walking habits. They were also provided with accelerometers to measure their physical activity levels over seven days.

The study revealed that individuals with a pet were, on average, active for an additional 30 minutes per day, exceeding the researchers' expectations.

The team recommends that physicians prescribe dog ownership or community dog-walking programs to older individuals to help them engage in more physical activity.

In an article published in the Journal of Epidemiology & Community Health, the researchers concluded that dog walking "may have considerable potential to support the maintenance of physical activity in older adults and could be included in exercise prescription programs."

The Head of World Cancer Research Fund, remarked, "It's uplifting to see that something as straightforward as dog walking can assist older individuals in being more physically active.

" She added, "Being physically active is extremely important. In fact, our own evidence has shown that it can help reduce the risk of developing a number of cancers including breast and bowel."

3 Read the text again and check (✓) the correct statement.

project

a. Researchers at the University of Cambridge found that people who walk dogs are more physically active, but have the same risks of developing cancer. ☐

b. Researchers at the University of Cambridge found that people who walk dogs are more physically active and have a lower risk of developing cancer. ☐

see word pop-up page 162

1 Work in groups of four. Form a sentence with as many words as you can. Pay attention to the example. Use the verbs in the box in the Present Perfect.

to work to study to travel to fly to clean

I have flown.

I have flown in a hot air balloon.

I have flown in a hot air balloon on the beach.

I have flown in a hot air balloon on the beach with my parents.

2 What's the meaning of "NANAND"?

How to play:

1. Work in groups of four.
2. Think about an activity that you have done for some time. For example: study.
3. Come up with sentences about this activity, replacing the activity with the word NANAND. *I have NANAND since 2010. I NANAND this morning.*
4. Your partners try to guess the meaning of NANAND. For example: *Does NANAND mean 'study'?*
5. The student who guesses the activity correctly gets one point.
6. Take turns. The first student to get four points is the winner.

3 You have two minutes to write a sentence with each verb below. Use the Present Perfect.

to be ______

to eat ______

to have ______

to read ______

to see ______

to write ______

Self-Assessment

Circle the correct option to complete the sentences.

1. We **lived/have lived** through situations you cannot even imagine.
2. **I've planned/planned** five lessons so far.
3. Laura **missed/has missed** two swimming classes last week.
4. Naomi's grandma is teaching **himself/herself** how to play the piano.
5. We really enjoyed **ourselves/yourself.** We danced a lot!
6. Angelina plays the flute **beautifully/beautiful**.
7. Anthony speaks German **well/goodly**.
8. It is difficult to understand Jeremy. He talks too **fastly/fast**.
9. Gymnasts can jump **really high/high quite**.
10. His car is not as fast as the other ones, but it is **quite fast/real fastly.**

What your score means...

8-10 Congratulations! You can understand and use the language learned in this unit.

5-7 Good job! How about looking back over pages 58 to 67? Then answer the questions again.

1-4 Oops... I'm sure you can do better! Let's try again! Go back to pages 58 to 67 and answer the questions. Ask your teacher for help.

Rewind 2 Units 3 - 4

1 Some teenagers from iLearn Middle School have just arrived at a summer camp. Look at the picture and complete the sentences with the verbs in parentheses.

a. Matheus has just arrived at the camp. (to arrive)

b. Andreza ______ just ______ swimming. (to go)

c. Paul ______ just ______ a race. (to win)

d. Tina and Josh ______ just ______ their bikes. (to ride)

e. Laura and Monica ______ just ______ a picnic. (to have)

f. Susan and some friends ______ just ______ soccer. (to play)

g. Josh and Milton ______ just ______ mangoes. (to eat)

h. Matt ______ just ______ 10 laps. (to swim)

2 Match the questions to the answers.

a. How long have you known her?

b. How long has she lived in this city?

c. How long has he played the guitar?

d. How long have they been here?

e. How long have you had a dog?

[ ] I've had a dog since I was a child.

[ ] He's played the guitar for two years.

[ ] I've known her for a year.

[ ] She's lived here since 2010.

[ ] They've been here since eight o'clock this morning.

3 Complete the sentences with the missing Reflexive Pronoun.

a. It's my opinion that music should not be free, and my prediction is that individual artists and their labels will someday decide what an album's price point is. I hope they don't underestimate __________ or undervalue their art.

b. This media company is reshaping __________ into a service provider that caters more directly to artists.

4 Now answer these questions with true information about you. Write complete answers.

a. Do you play any musical instruments?

____

b. How long have you studied at this school?

____

c. Have you ever taught yourself anything?

____

unit 5

I had just read a horror story.

IN THIS UNIT YOU WILL

- talk about past actions and identify which one happened first
- understand the difference between the Simple Past and the Past Perfect
- understand when to use adverbs of manner and frequency
- make comparisons using sense verbs

START UP

Let's plug in! What are the benefits of reading? Do you believe reading is the best form of self-educating? Share your ideas with your teacher and classmates.

LOADING

1 Listen to a voice message Eric sent his friend this morning and look at the pictures below.

27

2 Look at the pictures in Activity 1 and number the sentences in the box in the correct order.

- [ ] When I looked at her, she came over and rubbed up against my legs.
- [ ] I had just read a horror story and was ready to go to bed.
- [ ] I heard a noise.
- [ ] I slowly walked into the kitchen and opened the door.
- [ ] I went to the living room and turned on the lights.
- [1] My parents had already gone to bed.
- [ ] Our cat had eaten all the bananas my dad and I had bought in the morning.
- [ ] The neighbors had already turned off the lights.

Grammar feed

Past Perfect and Simple Past

Eric **heard** a noise **after** his parents **had gone** to bed.
2nd action — 1st action

By the time Eric **opened** the door, the cat **had eaten** all the bananas.
2nd action — 1st action

Before he **heard** a noise, he **had read** a horror story.
2nd action — 1st action

UPLOADING

3 **Underline the correct verb forms in the sentences below.**

a. Before Julia **arrived** / **had arrived** home, her mother **left** / **had left**.

b. Sam **tried** / **had tried** to call Gabi many times before he **texted** / **had texted** her.

c. Everyone **went** / **had gone** home by the time the cake **was** / **had been** ready.

d. After Nat **waited** / **had waited** for two hours, she **decided** / **had decided** to leave.

e. The bell **rang** / **had rung** by the time the students **sat** / **had sat** down.

f. When we **left** / **had left** to take the dog for a walk, we saw that he **ate** / **had eaten** his food.

4 **Look at the pictures. Then complete the sentences using the Past Perfect and the Simple Past.**

a.

When Alice arrived at home, she noticed that she had forgotten her keys. (to arrive / to forget)

b.

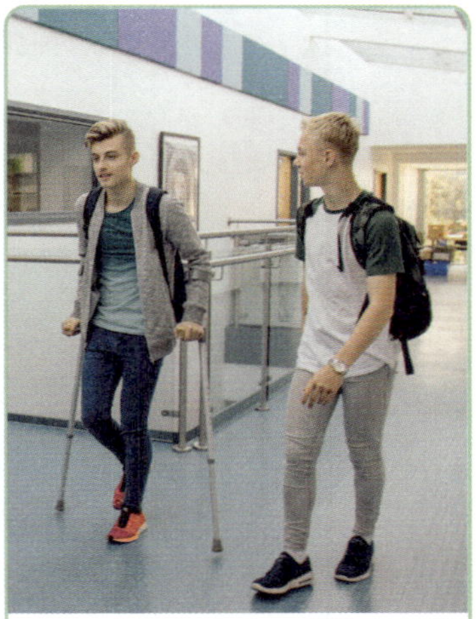

My friend Andrew ________ slowly because he ________ his leg. (to walk / to break)

c.

Jake ________ asleep before his friend ________ him. (to fall / to call)

DOWNLOADING

5 **Complete the sentence. Think of three situations that are true for your classmates.**

By the time the teacher arrived,

a. ________

b. ________

c. ________

Your turn!

Work with a partner and compare your sentences.

LOADING

1 Lizzie is talking to her father. Listen and read.

28

Dad: You look upset, Lizzie! What's wrong?

Lizzie: It's the movie I've just finished watching. I didn't like it.

Dad: What movie are you talking about, dear?

Lizzie: *Allegiant*.

Dad: *Allegiant?*

Lizzie: Yes… it's the third movie of *the Divergent Series*.

Dad: Oh, I see. Have you read the book?

Lizzie: Yes, I read it two weeks ago. Mom told me about it.

Dad: So, she had read the book before you, right?

Lizzie: Yes, and she liked it a lot, just like me.

Dad: Well, you know what they say: books are usually better than their movie version.

2 Complete the sentences with *before* or *after*.

a. Lizzie had watched the movie ___before___ she talked to her dad.

b. Lizzie read the book ________ her mom had read it.

c. Lizzie had read the book ________ she saw the movie.

3 Listen again and repeat the dialogue.

29

Grammar feed

Past Perfect: Questions

	Yes/No Questions	Question words
	Had Lizzie **seen** the movie before she read the book?	Who **had read** the book before Lizzie read it?
Affirmative:	Yes, she **had.**	Her mother **had read** it.
Negative:	No, she **hadn't.**	

UPLOADING

4 **Match the questions to the answers.**

a. Had you read any books by Richelle Mead before you got *Vampire Academy*?

b. How many drama movies had you seen before you saw *The Fault in Our Stars*?

c. What had the teacher asked the students to do before they failed the test?

d. Had they left by the time the school computer lab closed?

[ ] Yes, they left really early that day.

[ ] She had told them to study what they had seen the class before.

[ ] Yes, I had.

[ ] I had seen several, but this was my favorite.

5 **Complete the sentences with the Past Perfect or the Simple Past.**

a. **A:** [Had] she [lived] in many different places before she [moved] to Brazil? (to live / to move)

B: Yes, she [ ] in Mexico and in the United States. (to live)

b. **A:** Welcome back from your trip! How [ ] you [ ] Miami? (to like)

B: It [ ] great. (to be)

A: [ ] you [ ] there before? (to be)

B: No, I hadn't. It [ ] my first time there. (to be)

DOWNLOADING

6 **Imagine you had a very busy day yesterday. Complete the sentences with real or imaginary activities.**

a. I had already [ ] by 7:00 a.m.

b. By lunch time, I [ ].

c. By the end of the afternoon, I [ ].

d. By the time I went to bed, I [ ].

Your turn!

Work with a partner. Take turns asking and answering questions about the sentences in Activity 6.

What had you done by 7:00 a.m.?

I had made my bed and had breakfast. What about you? What had you done by that time?

I had taken a shower and walked my dog.

LOADING

1 **The 9th graders at iLearn Middle School have been interviewed about their reading habits for the school magazine. Read and listen to what two of them said in the interview.**

30

I really like reading, but print books, not e-books. I read almost every day. Last year I could read every day because school was not that hard. I read about two or three books a month. By the end of December, I had read 28 books in total. This year I read one book per month. And all of them are mine. I never borrow books. I prefer to buy them. I'm especially devoted to young adult fiction. I've read a lot of Amanda Hocking's books. I think she writes creatively.

I like reading, but I don't read very often. In my free time, I play different outdoor sports. I love online games, too. When I do read, I prefer e-books. They are quicker to get, take up less space, and don't use up trees. They're usually cheaper, too. I like fantasy stuff, but more like Narnia than Harry Potter. I had read *The Space Trilogy*, another series from C. S. Lewis, before I read *The Chronicles of Narnia* and I liked his writing style.

2 **Read the text again and check (✓) the true sentence(s).**

a. Both nine graders read very often. ☐

b. Sophia is more likely to read a book than Samuel. ☐

c. Both Sophia and Samuel prefer reading e-books to print books. ☐

Grammar feed

Adverbs of frequency and manner

Adverbs of frequency

Expressions of frequency usually go at the end of the sentence.

I read almost **every day**.

This year I have read **one book per month**.

Adverbs of frequency go **after** the verb *be* and **before** all the other verbs.

They're **usually** cheaper, too.

I **always** read young adult fiction books.

Adverbs of manner

Adverbs of manner are usually placed after the main verb or after the object.

I think she writes **creatively**.

He wrote scholarly books **well**.

UPLOADING

3 **Order the words to form sentences.**

a. usually / movies / books / she / watches / based on

She usually watches movies based on books.

b. read / they / print / rarely / books

c. often / buys / she / books

d. always / Pedro / first / in class / student / is / the

4 **Complete the sentences by changing the adjectives in parentheses into adverbs.**

a. Kobra is my favorite street artist. I think he paints beautifully. (beautiful)

b. We got there so ______ we even had time for a coffee. (quick)

c. "You're late!" my classmate said ______. "Where have you been?" (angry)

d. Manoela is sitting ______ at her desk. (quiet)

DOWNLOADING

5 **Write true sentences about you. Use an adverb of frequency.**

a. I study for seven hours a day.

I often study for seven hours a day.

b. I'm late for school.

c. I have English lessons.

LOADING

1 **Students from iLearn Middle School are attending their back-to-school night. Read the short dialogues and match them to the pictures.**

a. **A:** Your father looks like Beckham.
B: David Beckham? You must be kidding!

b. **A:** This cafeteria smells like chocolate.
B: Well, look around! There's chocolate everywhere.

c. **A:** Wow! This cake tastes like my grandma's cake.
B: Are you serious?

Study this

Using sense verbs to make comparisons:

Your father **looks like** Beckham.

This cafeteria **smells like** chocolate.

This cake **tastes like** my grandma's cake.

UPLOADING

2 **Complete the sentences with the correct form of *look*, *smell*, or *taste* + *like*.**

a. 

She ______ a princess!

b. 

This shampoo ______ coconut!

c. 

Her new car ______ a spaceship!

d. 

This pie ______ the ones my mom used to make when I was a child.

e. 

This chicken ______ coal! Eww!

f. 

This perfume ______ mine! It's a delicious scent!

3 **Write sentences with these prompts and a sense verb + *like*.**

a. Emma → her sister Emily

Emma looks like her sister Emily.

b. This ice cream → the one we bought in Argentina

______

c. Your perfume → the flowers in my mom's vase

______

DOWNLOADING

4 **Write true sentences with the sense verbs + *like*.**

a. ______

b. ______

c. ______

iSkills

iListen

1 **Listen to Ross talking about his trip to Paris and order the events.**

31

LEARNING STRATEGY

The Eiffel Tower

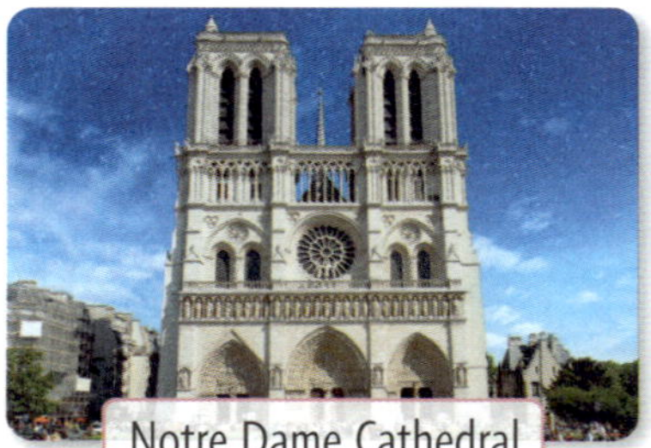
Notre Dame Cathedral

Luxembourg Gardens

☐ Ross visited Paris last year.

☐ Ross saved money for two years.

☐ Ross booked the trip.

☐ Ross read a few books about the city two months before the trip.

☐ Ross spent many days touring the city.

☐ Ross saw many beautiful places in Paris.

iWrite

2 **Make a list of your five favorite books.**

iSpeak

3 **Work with a partner. Which books from Activity 2 could be great movies? Talk about it with your partner and explain why.**

The Sense of an Ending could be a great movie. It's a stunning story about memory and friendship.

I agree.

I haven't read this book yet, but the story seems really interesting.

English for • *Literature*

1 **Have you watched the movie or read the play Romeo and Juliet by William Shakespeare? What is the story about?**

READING STRATEGY

iThink

2 **Read the story of Romeo and Juliet. Then match the columns.**

The 1996 movie version of *Romeo and Juliet* was a huge success and people love the story just as much today as when the play was first published in 1597!

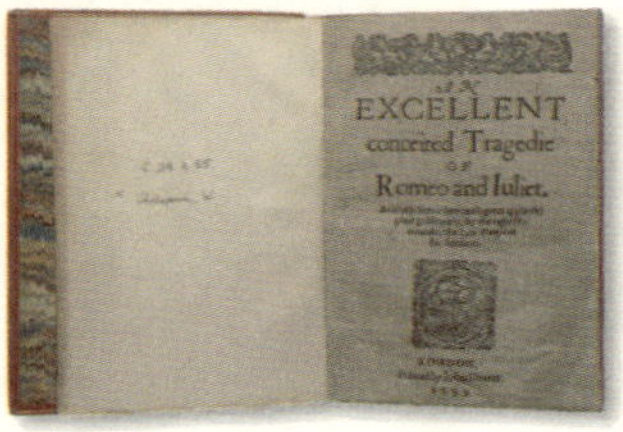

The story of Romeo and Juliet takes place in Verona, Italy. Two families, the Montagues and the Capulets, hate each other and fight all the time.

Romeo, 14, is the son of the Montague family. He and his friends decide that it would be exciting to go to a party the Capulets had organized for their daughter, who is almost 14, to meet her future husband. They go in disguise because if they are recognized at the party by the Capulets, they might be killed.

That night, at the party, Romeo meets Juliet, and they fall in love at first sight. However, Juliet's cousin, Tybalt, recognizes Romeo – he knows he is from the Montague family and wants to kill him. Romeo hides in the garden and talks to Juliet when she appears on her balcony. They realize that they are perfect for each other and decide to get married. The next day, they go to a priest called Friar Lawrence, who marries them in secret.

Tybalt starts a fight with Romeo's best friend. When Romeo steps in to break up the fight between the two men, his best friend is accidentally killed. Romeo runs after Tybalt and kills him. Romeo is sent away from Verona but Friar Lawrence, the priest who organized the secret wedding between Romeo and Juliet, arranges for them to see each other one more time.

Meanwhile, the Capulets decide that Juliet must marry Count Paris immediately. When Juliet says that she doesn't want to, her parents are very angry with her and her mother says she will never speak to her again. Of course, they do not know that she has already secretly married Romeo. Juliet asks Friar Lawrence to get her out of this difficult situation, so that she can see her beloved Romeo again. Friar Lawrence has an idea – he gives Juliet a drug to make everyone think she is dead, when in fact she's only in a long, deep sleep. While Juliet is sleeping, Friar Lawrence sends a message to Romeo to tell him to come to her tomb and take her away.

When the guests arrive for Juliet's wedding the next day, Juliet's lifeless body is discovered. Believing she is dead, her family put her in their tomb. Tragically, Romeo never gets Friar Lawrence's message that Juliet has taken a drug and is really alive, he only hears that she is dead. Romeo returns to Verona, and goes to Juliet's tomb. There, inside the tomb, he meets Count Paris, who has also come to say goodbye to Juliet. They fight and Romeo kills him. Romeo still believes that Juliet is dead, so he drinks poison and dies, but soon after this, Juliet wakes up. She sees that Romeo is dead, takes his knife and kills herself, too.

When the Capulets and Montagues discover that both their children are dead, they decide to make peace with each other and build a monument to the memory of both Romeo and Juliet.

a. The Montagues and the Capulets	[ ]	meet and fall in love.
b. Romeo and Juliet	[ ]	get married.
c. They secretly	[ ]	she sees that Romeo is dead and kills herself.
d. Juliet takes a drug	[ ]	hate each other, but in the end they make peace.
e. Romeo drinks poison	[ ]	because he thinks Juliet is really dead.
f. When Juliet wakes up,	[ ]	to make people think she's dead.

project

see word pop-up page 164

1 **There was a crime at a Thanksgiving party—someone stole the turkey. Read what the guests said about it.**

Mr. Wilson

I arrived at 10:00 p.m. When I arrived, some guests had already left and the turkey had already disappeared.

Ms. Martin

I arrived very early. It was 7:00 p.m. I was supposed to help set the table. But when I arrived, someone had already set the table. It was really weird.

Ms. Ferrari

I arrived at 9:00 p.m. I saw some people in the kitchen. Mr. Wilson, Mrs. Smith, and Miss Martin had already arrived. I don't remember seeing any other guests near the turkey, but I saw those three for sure.

Mrs. Smith

I arrived at 6:00 p.m. I saw the turkey roasting in the oven. I set the table. I think I was the first guest to arrive, no one had arrived yet.

Mr. Smith

My wife had arrived before me. I arrived a little late, around 9:30 p.m. I think the turkey had just disappeared. Everyone was tense. Mr. Wilson had already arrived; I saw his car near the front door.

2 **Now write the facts on the timeline. Give as many details as you can.**

6 p.m.	7 p.m.	9 p.m.	9:30 p.m.	10 p.m.
			The turkey was stolen.	

3 **In your opinion, who stole the turkey? How do you know?**

Self-Assessment

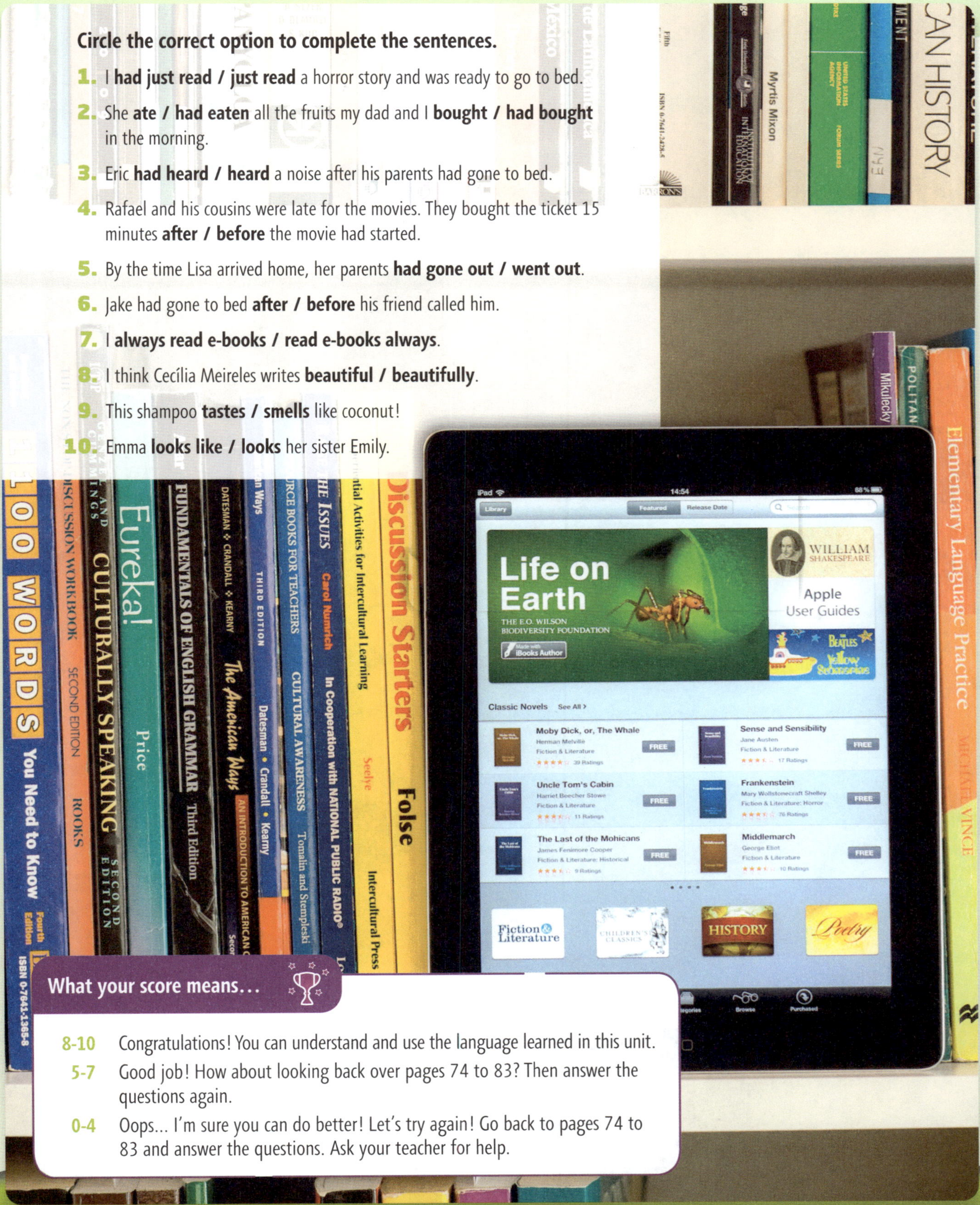

Circle the correct option to complete the sentences.

1. I **had just read / just read** a horror story and was ready to go to bed.
2. She **ate / had eaten** all the fruits my dad and I **bought / had bought** in the morning.
3. Eric **had heard / heard** a noise after his parents had gone to bed.
4. Rafael and his cousins were late for the movies. They bought the ticket 15 minutes **after / before** the movie had started.
5. By the time Lisa arrived home, her parents **had gone out / went out**.
6. Jake had gone to bed **after / before** his friend called him.
7. I **always read e-books / read e-books always**.
8. I think Cecília Meireles writes **beautiful / beautifully**.
9. This shampoo **tastes / smells** like coconut!
10. Emma **looks like / looks** her sister Emily.

What your score means...

8-10 Congratulations! You can understand and use the language learned in this unit.

5-7 Good job! How about looking back over pages 74 to 83? Then answer the questions again.

0-4 Oops... I'm sure you can do better! Let's try again! Go back to pages 74 to 83 and answer the questions. Ask your teacher for help.

unit 6 Moving away.

» IN THIS UNIT YOU WILL

- learn how to use the First Conditional to talk about possible future situations
- learn how to use prefixes and suffixes

START UP

Let's plug in! What can you see in the picture? What are the people doing? Do they look worried, relaxed, or happy?

LOADING

1 **Lauren studies in a bilingual school in Brazil. She is moving to the USA with her family soon, so she decided to write her school friends a farewell message on her social network page.**
32 **Listen and read what she wrote.**

Lauren

Lauren

Friends

Hi everyone,

I'm so excited, and at the same time so worried and sad! The reason is: the company where my father works is moving to Dallas, a city in Texas, and we're moving in a month. At first, Mom and Dad weren't sure whether moving abroad and starting a new life would be a good idea, but then they made up their minds. Dad feels that if he doesn't take advantage of this great opportunity now, he will not get the chance again. Personally, I think it will be difficult to adapt to a new school if my best friends are not around. I know I'll miss you all. I also need to concentrate on helping my grandparents. They are also moving with us, but they can't speak English. If we help them, they will learn a little of the language more quickly and do better in the U.S.

The good news is that my brothers can get a scholarship if they go on playing baseball well. Oh, and my mother is so excited about getting a new job and starting a different career! She said she won't complain about driving long hours to work if she has to. I'm not sure I believe her, but that's another story...

I want to say thank you to you all for the moments we shared in the last 9 years. Some of them were happy, sad, good, and bad, but I'll always remember them. Even though we'll be far away from each other, I know I can count on you if I ever have any problems or feel lonely. Thanks to the Internet, our friendship won't end if I don't come and visit you here in Brazil for a while.

I know you want to try to make me stay, but I can't. So, let's celebrate my moving away with a beautiful smile and a warm hug tomorrow morning!

Lauren.

25 likes   7 comments

2 **Read the text again and check (✓) the true sentences.**

a. In Lauren's opinion, her grandparents will do well in the U.S. even If they don't speak English. ☐

b. Lauren's mother is excited about starting a new career. ☐

c. Lauren's brothers are staying in Brazil with their grandparents because they're professional baseball players. ☐

d. If Lauren has any problems, she will talk to her friends on the Internet. ☐

3 **Read the post again. Underline the sentence that expresses the consequence if Lauren's father doesn't take the job.**

UPLOADING

Grammar feed

First Conditional

Present situation		Future consequence
If he **doesn't take** advantage of this great opportunity,	→	he **will not get** the chance again.
If we **help** them,	→	they **will learn** a little of the language more quickly.

If we **help** them, they **will learn** a little of the language more quickly. OR They **will learn** a little of the language more quickly if we **help** them.

Study this

will not = won't

4 **Match the present situations to their future consequences.**

a. If Lauren's brothers move to the U.S.A.,
b. If I study hard,
c. If Lauren invites me,
d. If it rains tomorrow,
e. If we don't go to bed now,

( ) I will get a good mark on the math test.
( ) we will feel sleepy tomorrow morning.
(a) they will probably play baseball for their college team.
( ) we won't have the picnic at the park.
( ) I might visit her in January.

5 **Julia, Lauren's classmate, is thinking about changing schools next year. Underline the correct words to complete the sentences.**

a. If I **change/will change** schools, I **study/will study** near my house.
b. If I **study/will study** near my house, I **have to get up/will have to get up** at 7:00 a.m.
c. If I **don't change/won't change** schools, my mom **has to/will have to** take me to school.
d. If my mom **has to/will have to** take me to school, she **is/will be** late for work every day.

6 **Complete the sentences with your own ideas.**

a. If I move to another country, ____________________.
b. If my friend doesn't tell me the truth, ____________________.
c. If the students don't do their homework, ____________________.

DOWNLOADING

7 **Lauren receives an envelope before she moves away and she does not know what is in it. Write what you think she will do with the contents of the envelope.**

a. If it is money, ____________________
____________________.
b. If it is a gift card from a store, ____________________
____________________.

Your turn!

Work with a partner. Compare your ideas.

LOADING

1 **Lauren will not visit her friends in Brazil next December, so they are planning to visit her in the U.S.A. Listen and read.**

33

Julia: Let's not tell Lauren that we are planning to visit her.

Paulo: I don't think that is a good idea. If we don't tell her, she will probably make other plans.

Ana: That's true. All right, we'd better tell her. But first we have to decide when we'll go.

Julia: Right. So, if we go in January, will the weather be hot or cold?

Paulo: It'll be cold. Besides, Lauren will have class in January…

Ana: Let's go in February then.

Julia: Not a good idea. She will have class, too. Besides, if we go in February, won't we miss class?

Paulo: Yes, we will. How about traveling during Carnival?

Ana: If we travel during Carnival, how many days will we spend there?

Julia: We'll have a week off school, so that will be perfect. What do you think?

Paulo: I think it is the best option. We can hang out with her when she is not in class. Now we need to talk to our parents and see if we can afford to travel. If we don't hurry, we won't get tickets to Dallas for that time.

2 **Read the dialogue again. Decide if the sentences are T (true) or F (false).**

a. Lauren's friends will miss class if they travel in February. [ ]

b. Paulo suggests traveling during Carnival, but the girls don't think it is a good idea. [ ]

c. Lauren's friends won't get the tickets in time if it takes them too long to decide. [ ]

d. They won't travel in January because they will start school that month. [ ]

3 **Answer the questions.**

a. If you can travel during school vacation, where will you go?

____

b. If we don't stop polluting the Earth, what will happen?

____

c. Will we save endangered species if we help protect our environment?

____

d. If I invite you to my party, will you come?

____

Grammar feed

First Conditional

Question with question words

If we travel during Carnival, **how many** days will we spend there?

If it is sunny on the weekend, **where** will we go?

***Yes/No* questions**

If we go in February, won't we miss classes?

Yes, we **will**.

If you come across your favorite singer, will you ask for a selfie?

No, I **won't**.

4 **Listen again and repeat the dialogue.**

34

UPLOADING

5 Complete the questions and the answers.

a. What will you study if you go to college? (to study)

I will probably study engineering. (to study)

b. _____ will the director call us if he _____ us to be in the play? (to want)

He _____ you during recess. (to call)

c. _____ the world _____ a better place if we start taking care of it right now? (to be)

Yes, it _____. What are we waiting for?

d. If your father _____ you travel, will you feel sad? (to let)

No, I _____. I'm sure he wants the best for me.

e. _____ will not come to school if it _____ heavily? (to rain)

I guess Anna _____ because she lives in the country. (not to come)

6 Unscramble the words and form questions. Then discuss the questions with a classmate.

a. future / how / our / will / affect / this

If artificially intelligent robots become part of our lives, how will this affect our future?

b. change / live / will / way / people / the / technology

_____ if we don't control it?

c. volunteer / where / you / will / your / and / classmates

_____ if your school lets you?

d. will / it / accept / you

If you get a scholarship to go to high school in Canada, _____?

DOWNLOADING

7 What will your future be like if you move away to another country? Write three true sentences using *will* and *won't*.

_____

_____

_____

Your turn!

Work with a partner. Ask him/her questions about possible situations in the future and take notes.

Then report your partner's answers to the class.

How will you celebrate if you pass this school grade?

Who will help you if you can't choose which high school to go to?

LOADING

1 **Read these testimonials from teens who moved abroad recently and number the pictures.**

a. "I was unhappy because I thought I would lose touch with my friends back home."

b. "My parents were dissatisfied with my performance in the first history test I took the year we moved away. The problem was, because I couldn't write in English very well, my teacher misunderstood my answer to the question."

c. "I was sad because I couldn't adjust to the new culture after my father was reallocated in his job."

d. "My younger brother and I were happy to move to a country where we could have an extraordinary future."

2 **Listen and repeat the sentences.**

35

Grammar feed

Prefixes: added to the beginning of a word

Prefixes	Meanings	Examples
anti-	against	antibiotic
co-	with	co-worker
dis-	not	dissatisfied
extra-	more than	extraordinary
mis-	wrongly	misunderstood
pre-	before	preview
re-	again	readjust
un-, im-, ir-	opposite	unhappy, impossible, irregular

3 **Write three sentences using three prefixes from the list above. Write them on the lines below.**

UPLOADING

4 **Choose the most suitable prefix to form new words and complete the sentences.**

a. Jerry was very ☐ responsible when he didn't warn the school about his leaving.

☐ ir- ☐ mis-

b. The teacher told me that if I ☐ write my essays, I will improve my skills.

☐ un- ☐ re-

c. If our neighbors don't ☐ operate, our park will never be clean.

☐ anti- ☐ co-

d. If you don't clarify the information, people may ☐ interpret you.

☐ pre- ☐ mis-

e. The reasons why he didn't move away are ☐ clear.

☐ un- ☐ extra-

5 **Use a word from the box to complete the captions. Then circle the prefixes.**

underwear unhappy overweight

a.

He is ______.

b.

This man is ______.

c.

They've washed their ______.

DOWNLOADING

6 **Work with a partner. Choose 3 prefixes. Write down as many words as you can remember with each prefix. You have 3 minutes for each prefix!**

______

______

______

LOADING

LEARNING STRATEGY

1 Read the text and pay close attention to the words in bold.

Living Abroad

Living in a foreign country can change your life in many ways. The opportunity to explore the world and immerse yourself in a different culture is **incredible**, leaving you with memories that will last a lifetime. Many people who have lived abroad look back with **fondness** on the lessons they learned, the people they met, and the adventures they experienced.

However, not everyone enjoys living abroad. Some people move to a new country thinking it will solve all their problems, but they go in with **unrealistic** expectations and **assumptions**. When these aren't met, they may struggle with the challenges of living in a new place and quickly want to return home.

The **difference** between a rewarding experience and a difficult one often depends on how well you prepare before moving overseas. It's important not to rush into the decision, as proper preparation can help you avoid many of the common difficulties people face.

2 Match the words in bold from the text to their definitions.

a. ______ : adj. not reasonable

b. ______ : *noun* opposite of *similarity*

c. ______ : *noun* the same as *affection*

d. ______ : *adj.* extremely good

e. ______ : *noun* something that you think is true although you have no definite proof

Grammar feed

Suffixes: added to the end of a word

Suffixes	Meanings	Examples
-ence	state or condition	difference
-er	person or object that does a specified action	teacher
-ible	able to be	incredible
-ic	relating to, characterized by	unrealistic
-ify, -fy	make or become	justify
-ion	quality or state	assumption
-ness	quality or state (forms nouns)	fondness
-ship	skill of, state or condition of	friendship

Study this

Common suffixes for nouns: *-ment, -ism, -ness, -ship, -er/-or, -tion*

Common suffixes for verbs: *-ate, -ify, -ise/-ize*

Common suffixes for adjectives: *-able, -al, -ful, -ous/-ious, -ive*

Common suffixes for adverbs: *-ly, -ward/-wards, -wise*

UPLOADING

3 **Jonathan used to be Lauren's classmate. He's moved away with his family recently. He's calling Lauren to talk about his new city. Listen to their conversation and check (✓) the problems he mentions.**

36

4 **Add a suffix from the list to the words in parentheses to replace the underlined ones. Then rewrite the sentences extracted from the conversation.**

~~-ible~~ -able -ful -hood

a. "The streets are <u>terrible</u>." (horror)

The streets are horrible.

b. "So, how do you like your new <u>town</u>?" (neighbor)

c. "I need some <u>nice</u> tips to make friends there." (use)

d. "I will make sure you have a more <u>pleasant</u> experience." (enjoy)

DOWNLOADING

5 **Work with a partner. Talk about your future using the topics in the box. Remember to use suffixed words in your conversation.**

adapt to a new culture
make new friends
move to another city
visit a friend who lives abroad

Your turn!

Share your ideas with the whole group.

iRead

1 How do you keep in touch with your family and friends? How do you think people used to communicate in the 1990s?

2 Read the article below and find out if your answer to question 1 matches the author's opinions. READING STRATEGY

Staying Connected:

Communicating from Abroad Has Never Been Easier

Using a gadget such as a laptop or your own telephone overseas to communicate back home is commonplace now.

It was 1990. I was 17 years old, 5,000 miles away from home and desperately wishing I could easily communicate with my friends and family. But there were only two options: novel-length letters or POTS (Plain Old Telephone Service). Now, in the 21st century, keeping in contact when you are abroad has become a breeze.

[...]

Moving beyond POTS

In the 20th century a land line telephone was the quickest and most expensive way to say "hello." Still one of the fastest forms of verbal interaction, the phone has become a cost-effective means of communication.

The big step towards cheap, long distance telephone service was the development of VoIP (Voice Over Internet Protocol). VoIP is based on the concept that sound bites travel through high speed Internet connections in the same way an e-mail does, creating a clear telephone connection. The lightning fast exchange of information supports conversations with any other type of phone, whether or not it is a POTS. The only requirement is for your phone or computer to be connected to WiFi or a data port.

[...]

The other direction taken towards cheaper communication over the phone involved a program that is easily downloaded to any computer. Skype has taken advantage of VoIP technology by creating a program that supports various forms of communication when it is downloaded to a PC or Mac. [...]

The Internet

The increasing feasibility of real-time communication would not be possible without the Internet. Luckily for today's traveler, Internet cafés, and WiFi hot spots are a common occurrence everywhere. Quality computer notebooks have hit prices below U$500 making it more financially feasible to own one.

[...]

Another way to reach the masses is writing a blog. A blog has different services. One is using it as a virtual post card. It can be used as a basic diary, helping your loved ones know your travel story. The only difference being that your readers can respond to your letters instantly. Another is the sharing of information; creating a place for people to learn about a unique aspect to your life abroad. [...]

For those living abroad or thinking about doing so, the communication options of today make the process much easier. It truly is a small world. Thanks to technology, keeping in touch is just as easy, no matter if you are close by or far away. And while you are abroad it is nice to know that loved ones are no farther than the push of a button; a convenience that is important for both the person venturing out into the world and those left behind.

iThink

see word pop-up page 170

3 The writer compares communication in the past to communication in the present. Refer to the text again and underline 2 sentences that show this contrast.

English for • Culture

1 In your opinion, what is the most popular destination for Brazilians in the United States?

2 Listen and read the article to confirm your guesses.

37

Brazilians in the United States

SPOTLIGHT

A sign for Little Brazil Street in Times Square. The New York City metropolitan area is home to the largest number of Brazilian immigrants in the United States. (Photo: Diego Torres Silvestre)

Brazilian migration to the United States—a relatively small flow until recent decades—began to grow significantly in the early 1980s, driven in large part by a series of economic crises in Brazil. The Brazilian immigrant population in the United States doubled during the 1980s, almost tripled in the 1990s, and then stabilized following the Great Recession of 2007-09 [...]. In 2014, 336,000 Brazilian immigrants lived in the United States, representing 1 percent of the 42.4 million immigrants in the country. Approximately one-fifth to one-third of them are in the United States without authorization, according to Migration Policy Institute (MPI) estimates.

Economic and social conditions in Brazil, together with changes in U.S. immigration policy, have shaped the nature and scope of the Brazilian flow to the United States. [...]

In recent years, factors including economic recession in the United States, stepped up U.S. immigration enforcement, and improved economic prospects in Brazil have led a significant number of immigrants to return to Brazil, especially those who are unauthorized and/or employed in low-skilled jobs. Meanwhile, the number of Brazilian international students in the United States has more than tripled, from 7,000 in 2005 to 24,000 in 2015—in part thanks to increased investment by the Brazilian government in international scholarships.

While the United States is the top destination for Brazilian migrants, less than one-quarter of the 1.5 million Brazilian emigrants live in the United States. Others reside in Japan (182,000), Portugal (130,000), and Italy (104,000), according to mid-2015 estimates by the United Nations Population Division. [...]

Most Brazilian immigrants who obtain lawful permanent residence in the United States (also known as receiving a green card) qualify as immediate relatives of U.S. citizens. Compared to the total foreign-born population, Brazilian immigrants are less likely to be Limited English Proficient (LEP), have higher educational attainment and income, and have lower poverty rates.

[...]

In the 2010-14 period, the U.S. cities with the greatest number of Brazilian immigrants were the New York City, Boston, and Miami metropolitan areas. These three metropolitan areas accounted for about 41 percent of Brazilian immigrants in the United States.

[...]

see word pop-up page 170

project

rePlay

1 **Look at the pictures below. Imagine what the people are saying and write captions.**

a.

If she doesn't pay attention to the street,

she will get run over by a car.

c.

If you don't eat salad,

e.

If I don't hurry,

b.

If she falls,

d.

If you don't study,

f.

If you don't clean your room,

2 **Work in groups of four and prepare a speech for an election for class president. The team that makes the best promises is the winner.**

Self-Assessment

Circle the correct option to complete the sentences.

1. If you help me with my homework, I **will finish/finish** it faster.
2. Dad won't have time to visit Granny if he **will work/works** late tonight.
3. What **will you tell/you will tell** Sally if you meet her outside?
4. If Boon **will eat/eats** all his dinner, will his mom give him the dessert?
5. Who will carry on the luggage if the bellboy **won't be/isn't** around?
6. Lauren thinks her grandparents might have problems with the language, but I **disagree/agreeable**.
7. Karson texted us to **justification/justify** his awful attitude last night.
8. Keeping **friendships/unfriend** is one of the challenges of moving abroad.
9. Those are really **comfortably/comfortable** shoes. Let's pack them!
10. The number of **illegal/illegally** immigrants in the U.S. is greater than I had expected.

What your score means…

- **8-10** Congratulations! You can understand and use the language learned in this unit.
- **5-7** Good job! How about looking back over pages 88 to 97? Then answer the questions again.
- **0-4** Oops... I'm sure you can do better! Let's try again! Go back to pages 88 to 97 and answer the questions. Ask your teacher for help.

Rewind 3 Units 5 - 6

1 Match the columns and form sentences.

a. By the time Mom arrived home,
b. When I met Julio,
c. Marcello came to America
d. She had seen the movie
e. When the bell rang,
f. When I took out the trash,
g. By the time I arrived with the cake,

[ ] all the students had already left the school.
[ ] after he had lived in Paris.
[ ] before I told her about it.
[ ] he had already graduated.
[a] I had done my homework.
[ ] I saw that my mom had thrown away lots of plastic bags.
[ ] she had made a cake herself for her brother.

2 Rewrite the sentences below using an adverb from the box.

terribly happily loudly well wonderfully

a. They sang Italian songs.

______

b. The children laughed.

______

c. My sister plays the guitar.

______

3 Complete the sentences with the verbs in parentheses so that they express possible situations.

a. You won't pass if you don't study harder. (to study)
b. Elephants will become extinct if we ______ them. (to protect)
c. If I make some coffee, how many cups ______ you ______? (to drink)
d. You ______ see it better if you turn on the lights. (to be able to)
e. She will look completely different if she ______ her hair cut that way. (to have)

4 Underline the nouns with prefixes or suffixes in the sentences below.

a. I'm sure you have taken antibiotics at least once in your lifetime.
b. He has been my co-worker since 2002.
c. Happiness is much more important than money.
d. The party gave us a chance to renew old friendships.
e. She has worked there as a history teacher for over ten years.

5 Read the text. Then read the sentences and check (✓) the correct one(s).

Being an emotionally healthy person requires that you develop meaningful relationships outside of your family circle. If you're like most millennials, social media is a tool you use for making new personal connections.
Studies have shown that people mostly use social media sites like Facebook because they meet the basic need of connecting to others: making friends, keeping up with their lives, and updating friends on your own life.
While sites like Facebook were designed to connect people online who already knew each other offline, most people using them have formed connections with people they didn't know outside of Facebook. That's particularly the case with millennials.
But how does social media impact the quality of friendships among members of this generation? Like gambling and substance abuse, the need for attention via likes or comments can quickly become addictive and cause controversy between friends. In fact, research has shown that 42% of social media users admit to feeling jealous when a friend's posts receive more attention than theirs.

a. People have made friends on social media sites they didn't know before, but that was not the original intention of those sites. ☐

b. Millennials are the only people who use social media sites to connect with people they didn't know outside of them. ☐

c. Very few social media users admit to feeling jealous when a friend's posts receive more attention than theirs. ☐

6 Answer these questions. Use true information about you.

a. Do you like reading print books or e-books?

b. How many books do you read per month?

c. Which Brazilian author writes the most creatively?

d. Will you miss classes if you travel in February?

e. Will your parents be worried if you arrive home late today?

f. Will you wash the dishes if a friend cooks dinner for you?

unit

7 If I had one wish...

» IN THIS UNIT YOU WILL

- talk about hypothetical and imaginary situations
- compare First and Second Conditional sentences
- use Tag questions to confirm information

START UP

Let's plug in! What can you see in the picture? What are the teenagers in the picture thinking of? Share your answers with your teacher and classmates.

LOADING

1 (38) **Listen and read these teenagers' posts on an Internet forum. They all answer the question "What would you do if you were the president of your country?"**

iLEARN TEEN FORUM

HOME | FORUM | REGISTER

Thread: What would you do if you were the president of your country?

December 6, 9:30

Iza

In my opinion, citizens' voices are never heard. If I were the president of my country, I wouldn't ignore the people; on the contrary, I would make sure to meet their needs.

December 6, 11:00

Tracy

That's a tough one. Let me see... I have always thought governors should not rule alone. If I won the election, I wouldn't govern by myself. In my government, citizens would be encouraged to participate more actively in community projects.

December 7, 10:47

Sérgio

Well, I would like people to care more about making our town greener. I would start campaigns to encourage citizens not to litter and keep their surroundings clean if I had the chance to be the president of my country.

December 8, 8:03

Lizzie Anne

There are many things that are wrong in my country. I don't like the poor quality of the bike lanes available in most cities. If I had the chance to become the president of my country, I would invest in better infrastructure and show my fellow citizens the benefits of urban cycling.

2 (39) **Listen and read the posts again. The teenagers mention some things they are not satisfied with and would change. Underline the sentences that explain the reasons why they would make these changes.**

NEW iLearn ENGLISH

The Science of Love

Renata Chimim
Illustrated by Raoni Marqs

Pearson

Pearson

MISTO
Papel | Apoiando o manejo florestal responsável
FSC® C103535

Head of Product - Pearson Brasil	Gabriela Diuana
Product Manager - Pearson Brasil	Marjorie Robles
Product Coordinator - ELT	Mônica Bicalho
Author	Renata Chimim
Teacher's Guide	Gisele Aga
Editor - ELT	Renata S. C. Victor
Editorial Assistant - ELT	Simara Dal'Alba (Allya Assessoria Linguística)
Proofreader (English)	Rhiannon Ball
Copyeditor	Maria Estela Alcântara
Art and Design Manager	Cleber Carvalho
Art Editor - ELT	Emily Andrade
Acquisitions and permissions Manager	Maiti Salla
Acquisitions and permissions team	Cristiane Gameiro Heraldo Colon Maricy Queiroz Sandra Sebastião Shirlei Sebastião
Graphic design	Mirella Della M. Armentano Apis Design Integrado
Graphic design (cover)	Apis Design Integrado
Production Editors	Daniel Reis Vitor Marins
Illustrated by	Raoni Marqs
Media Development	Estação Gráfica
Audio	Maximal Studio

Printed in Brazil by Reproset RPPA 222127

Dados Internacionais de Catalogação na Publicação (CIP)
(Câmara Brasileira do Livro, SP, Brasil)

Índices para catálogo sistemático:
1. Inglês : Ensino fundamental 372.652

Índices para catálogo sistemático:
1. Inglês : Ensino fundamental 372.652

ISBN 9788543024455

2018

IN SCIENCE CLASS
A COCKTAIL OF CHEMICALS CAN MIX TWO ELEMENTS TOGETHER.
THEY MIGHT NOT GET ALONG WELL AND STILL BE SEPARATED.
THEY MIGHT NOT GET ALONG AT ALL.
OR THEY MIGHT BLEND TOGETHER SO WELL...
...THAT YOU CAN'T SEE EACH OF THEM SEPARATELY ANYMORE.

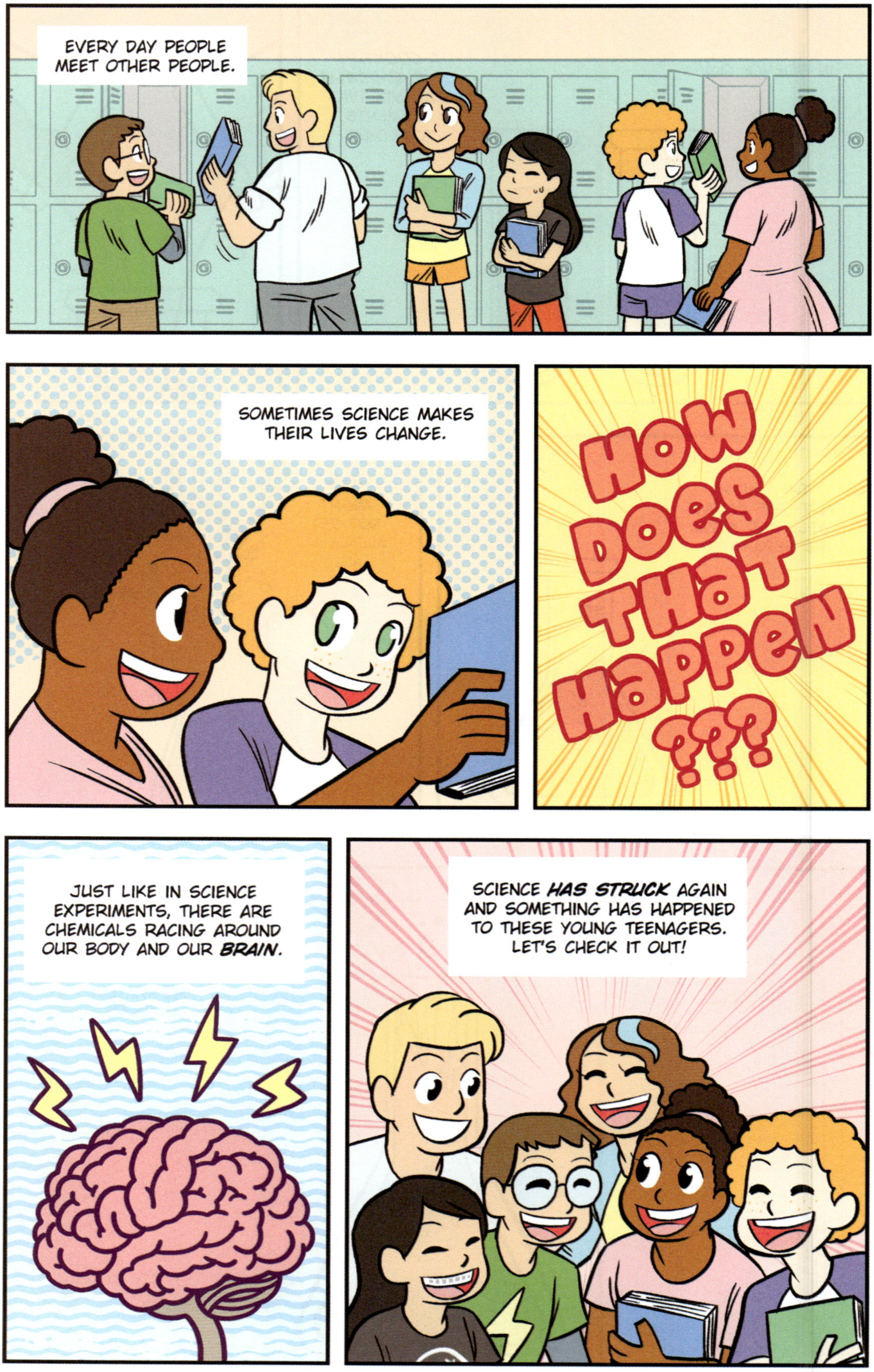
EVERY DAY PEOPLE MEET OTHER PEOPLE.
SOMETIMES SCIENCE MAKES THEIR LIVES CHANGE.
HOW DOES THAT HAPPEN???
JUST LIKE IN SCIENCE EXPERIMENTS, THERE ARE CHEMICALS RACING AROUND OUR BODY AND OUR *BRAIN*.
SCIENCE ***HAS STRUCK*** AGAIN AND SOMETHING HAS HAPPENED TO THESE YOUNG TEENAGERS. LET'S CHECK IT OUT!

HEY GIRLS, DID YOU GET AN INVITATION TO GABRIEL'S BIRTHDAY PARTY?
YES, I DID.
I DIDN'T. LET ME SEE IT.
CELEBRATE THIS SPECIAL DATE WITH ME! COME TO MY BIRTHDAY PARTY NEXT SATURDAY AT MY HOUSE AT 6 P.M.
I CAN'T WAIT TO SEE YOU THERE!
GABRIEL

I THINK GABRIEL IS SO *CUTE*!
COME ON... HE'S OUR FRIEND.
SO WHAT? HE IS OUR FRIEND AND HE IS CUTE.
YEP, JUST LIKE ADAM. DON'T YOU AGREE, CAMILLA?
WHAT ARE YOU TRYING TO SAY?
ADAM IS CUTE, TOO.
AND HE'S VERY INTELLIGENT AND FUNNY AT THE SAME TIME. THE PERFECT MATCH FOR...
ALL RIGHT, ALL RIGHT. I GET IT. WE WERE TALKING ABOUT GABRIEL'S BIRTHDAY. ARE YOU ALL GOING TO THE PARTY?
WE SURE ARE!

THE NEXT DAY IN SCIENCE CLASS
SWEATY HANDS, RACING HEART AND FLUSHED SKIN, ARE SOME OF THE PHYSICAL REACTIONS PEOPLE HAVE WHEN THEY FALL IN LOVE.
DOES ANYONE KNOW WHAT CAUSES THESE?
THAT'S EASY! THE CAUSE IS A BEAUTIFUL AND SMART GIRL.
WELL, IT MIGHT START WITH THIS GIRL, HENRY. RESEARCHERS SAY THAT WHEN YOU LOOK AT THIS SPECIAL GIRL, THERE IS A CHEMICAL REACTION IN THE BRAIN.
I THOUGHT WE LOVED WITH OUR HEARTS AND NOT WITH OUR BRAINS.
THE HEART IS THE SYMBOL OF LOVE, BUT OUR BODY'S REACTIONS COME FROM OUR BRAIN.

DOPAMINE PRODUCES A FEELING OF *BLISS* AND NOREPINEPHRINE,
Dopamine + Norepinephrine
WHICH IS SIMILAR TO ADRENALINE, PRODUCES THE RACING HEART.
HEY, ADAM, WHO IS THIS BOY HENRY?
OH... HE IS THE NEW STUDENT.
TOMORROW WE WILL TALK MORE ABOUT THE BRAIN.

AT CAMILLA'S HOUSE
LOOK, GIRLS! I FOUND HIM! THAT'S HIS PROFILE.
YOU'RE REALLY INTERESTED IN THIS NEW GUY, AREN'T YOU?
WHY DON'T YOU ADD HIM?
YES, THAT'S A GOOD IDEA! ADD HIM AND INVITE HIM TO GO TO GABRIEL'S PARTY WITH YOU.
NO, I WON'T INVITE HIM. I'LL ADD HIM AND THAT'S ALL.
BUT THERE'S SOMETHING STRANGE HAPPENING. I THINK I'M FEELING EXACTLY HOW THE TEACHER EXPLAINED IN OUR CLASS TODAY.
LOVE IS IN THE AIR!

AT THE GYM
SO, WHERE DID YOU STUDY BEFORE?
I WAS AT A SCHOOL IN CHICAGO.
CHICAGO? SO YOU **MUST** BE HAPPY WITH THE WEATHER HERE IN NEW YORK. IT IS VERY SIMILAR TO CHICAGO.
YEP. I LIKE THE COLD WEATHER.
HEY, IT'S MY BIRTHDAY THIS SATURDAY AND I'M GOING TO ***THROW A PARTY***. DO YOU WANT TO COME?
COOL! THANKS FOR THE INVITATION.
WILL CHLOE BE THERE?
?
SHE MIGHT BE.

I'VE JUST ADDED HER ONLINE.
SHE'S PRETTY AND **SEEMS** COOL.
WHAT ABOUT YOU? DO YOU HAVE A GIRLFRIEND?
NO, I DON'T WANT TO FALL IN LOVE. I WANT TO FOCUS ON MY STUDIES.
ME TOO!
?

MEANWHILE...
SCIENCE IS STARTING TO ACT. ELEMENTS ARE ABOUT TO BE MIXED TOGETHER.
ARE THEY GOING TO BLEND *NATURALLY*?
henry
Henry
Henry:
Were you at the mall today?
Chloe:
Yes, I was. You had just left when I got there.
Henry:
Are you going to Gabriel's party tomorrow?
Chloe:
Henry:
I'll see you there then.
WILL THAT CAUSE A REACTION IN THE BRAIN?
Henry
Henry:
Were you at the mall today?
Henry:

SATURDAY HAS ARRIVED!
CAMILLA, HELP ME WITH THIS, PLEASE! I DON'T KNOW WHAT TO WEAR TONIGHT!
WHAT'S HAPPENED TO YOU, CHLOE? YOU DON'T USUALLY WEAR THOSE KINDS OF CLOTHES.
WELL, IT'S A PARTY AND PEOPLE WEAR CLOTHES LIKE THIS. AND... AND...
AND WHAT?
HENRY IS GOING TO BE THERE!
OH... NOW I GET IT... BUT HE MET YOU WEARING JEANS AND T-SHIRT AND HE LIKED YOU LIKE THAT.
THAT'S THE REAL CHLOE. DON'T TRY TO BE SOMEONE ELSE NOW. THAT IS NOT YOU!
YOU'RE RIGHT.

I WONDER ABOUT THE BOYS. DO THEY WORRY ABOUT WHAT THEY LOOK LIKE JUST LIKE WE DO?
I DON'T THINK SO.
CAMILLA, WHAT ABOUT YOU? AREN'T YOU *NERVOUS*?
NERVOUS ABOUT WHAT?
YOU MIGHT MEET A CUTE BOY THERE. OR YOU MIGHT *REALIZE* THAT GABRIEL IS YOUR *PRINCE CHARMING.*
OH... STOP SAYING THAT! HE'S JUST A FRIEND.
A GOOD FRIEND...

PARTY TIME!
HI, HENRY! HOW ARE YOU?
I'M GREAT, THANKS! HEY, LET ME INTRODUCE YOU TO MONICA.
YOU TWO LOOK ALIKE, DON'T YOU THINK SO? ISN'T MONICA *CUTE*?
BUT WHO IS SHE? IS SHE YOUR...?
MY GIRLFRIEND? NO. WE'VE JUST MET.
EVERYBODY IS GORGEOUS ACCORDING TO HENRY. I'M NOT SPECIAL ANYMORE. I DON'T THINK WE'RE GOING TO GET ALONG WELL...

HEY THERE! IT'S SO NICE TO SEE EVERYONE HERE! GABRIEL IS GOING TO BE SO HAPPY!
THAT'S WHAT FRIENDS ARE FOR!
RAM... RAM... RAM...
EERR... YEAH... FRIENDS... YOU LOOK... YOU LOOK...
GORGEOUS!
OH... WAS CHLOE RIGHT ABOUT ADAM?
I FELT SOMETHING STRANGE JUST THEN.

HAPPY BIRTHDAY, GABRIEL!
THANK YOU, EVERYONE! THE PARTY HAS JUST STARTED! HAVE FUN!

HE'S CUTE AND HE'S A GOOD FRIEND.
EVERY DAY PEOPLE MEET OTHER PEOPLE.
AND SOMETIMES WE FEEL DIFFERENTLY ABOUT PEOPLE WE ALREADY KNOW.
WE ARE JUST SCIENCE EXPERIMENTS, WAITING TO FIND THE CORRECT COMBINATION OF CHEMICALS.
IT MIGHT HAPPEN TODAY OR IT MIGHT NOT. BUT, EVENTUALLY, IT WILL HAPPEN.
THE END.

Word pop-up

to add - adicionar
anxious - ansioso/a
to blend - misturar; mistura
bliss - felicidade; alegria; contentamento
brain - cérebro
chemicals - produtos/ substâncias químicas
cocktail - coquetel
Come on! - Vamos lá!
cool - legal, bacana
cute - bonito/a
to cut - cortar
flushed skin - corado; ruborizado
to get along - se dar bem
gorgeous - lindo/a; deslumbrante
match - combinação
must - dever, ter que
naturally - naturalmente
nervous - nervoso/a
prince charming - príncipe encantado
profile - perfil
racing heart - coração disparado
reactions - reações
to realize - perceber
researchers - pesquisadores
to seem - parecer
smart - inteligente
so what? - e daí?
struck - passado de *to strike*, suscedeu, ocorreu
sweaty - suado/a
still - ainda
to throw a party - dar/ oferecer uma festa

UPLOADING

Grammar feed

Second Conditional

Real Situation	Hypothetical Situation	Consequence
Citizens' voices are never heard.	**If** I **were** the president of my country,	I **wouldn't ignore** the people.
Governors should not rule alone.	**If** I **won** the election,	I **wouldn't govern** by myself.
People don't care much about having a green town.	**If** I **had** the chance to be the president of my country,	I **would start** campaigns to encourage citizens not to litter.

Study this

Contractions

would = **'d**

would not = **wouldn't**

3 Read the sentences. Then circle the correct answer.

a. If I **were/would** the president, I **encouraged/would encourage** people to participate more in community projects in my country, such as volunteer at a soup kitchen or organize activities for children in hospitals.

b. I **got/would get** up at 6 every day if I **had/would have** to attend meetings early in the morning.

c. If I **had/would have** more free time, I **read/would read** more about politics.

d. If I **met/would meet** a famous person on the street, I **didn't take/wouldn't take** a picture.

4 Complete the first clauses with the correct form of the verb in parentheses. Then match them to the second clauses.

a. If I were (to be) a politician, — [ ] if there wasn't any violence in the world.

b. If I ______ (to have) a magic wand, — [ ] I would live on a private island.

c. If I ______ (to be) the richest person in the world, — [a] I would be respectful to the citizens.

d. If computers ______ (not to exist), — [ ] my job would be much more difficult.

e. Everyone's lives ______ (to be) much better — [ ] I would put an end to famine and disease.

DOWNLOADING

5 Choose three clauses from Activity 4. Complete them with your own ideas.

______

______

______

Your turn!

Work in groups of three.
Share your sentences from Activity 5 with your classmates.

LOADING

1 **Terry, Paula, and Andrea are answering a quiz from an online teen magazine. Listen and read.**

40

Paula: Look! Here's a personality quiz about what we would do in some odd situations. Let's take it.

Terry: What do you mean by "odd"?

Paula: They're talking about hypothetical situations, things that are unusual or probably not likely to happen.

Andrea: That sounds interesting. What's the first question?

Paula: "If you had a super power, which super power would you have? A be invisible, B turn things into gold, or C fly." What do you think?

Andrea: Hmm... I think I would choose C. I would love it if I could fly like a bird.

Paula: What about you, Terry? Would you choose to fly, too?

Terry: No, I wouldn't. I would go for being invisible. If I were invisible, I would be able to go anywhere and no one would even notice me! How cool is that?

Paula: Well, I would like to turn things into gold. That way I could also help end poverty. I would use the gold to buy food for poor families.

Andrea: We all have different answers. Let's see the result.

Paula: OK. All we have to do is answer 54 more questions and...

Andrea: 54 questions?! Forget it!

2 **Read the dialogue again. Then circle the correct answer.**

a. The quiz is about **common/strange** situations.

b. There are **three/four** options for the first question.

c. The teenagers don't have **different/similar** answers.

d. The quiz has **more than/fewer than** 50 questions.

e. According to the dialogue, the next questions involve **real/hypothetical** situations as well.

3 **Listen and repeat the dialogue.**

41

UPLOADING

Grammar feed

Second Conditional

Questions with question words	Yes/No questions
If you had a super power, **which** super power **would** you have?	**If** you could have a super power, **would** you choose being able to fly? **Yes**, I would. **No**, I wouldn't.

Study this

In Second Conditional sentences *If I/he/she/it were* is more common than *If I/he/she/it was*.

4 Answer the questions.

a. If you could be a different person for one day, who would you choose to be?

b. What costume would you wear if you went to a costume party?

c. Would you give autographs if you were famous?

d. If you won a million dollars, how would you spend it?

5 Use the words to write questions.

a. If you (to find) some money on the street / you (to keep) it?

If you found some money on the street, would you keep it?

b. What you (to do) / if your neighbor (to play) loud music in the middle of the night?

c. If you (can) live in another country, / where you (to like) to live?

DOWNLOADING

6 Work with a partner. Take turns asking and answering the questions you wrote in Activity 5.

If you found some money on the street, would you take it?

Yes, I would. I wouldn't use the money. I would take it to the nearest police station.

LOADING

1 **Read the definition below. Can you explain the meaning of the word *poll* in your own words?**

LEARNING STRATEGY

2 **Answer the following poll questions.**

?

If you had a time machine, would you visit your past or future?

- [ ] I'd visit my past, because I'd love to revisit old favorite memories.
- [ ] I'd visit my future, because I'd love to see where I'll be in five or ten years.

?

If you pass all your exams this year, will you...

- [ ] change schools next year?
- [ ] stay at the same school?

3 **Ask your classmates about their answers to the poll questions in Activity 2. Then write the results of the poll in the box below.**

______ students would visit their past, while ______ would visit their future.
______ students will change schools next year, while ______ will stay at the same school.

UPLOADING

4 **Decide whether the situations below are possible (P) or hypothetical (H). Then complete the gaps accordingly.**

a. If you [had] (to have) a time machine, when and where would you travel to? [H]

b. How [ ] you [ ] (to fight) prejudice at school if you were the principal? [ ]

c. Will we arrive on time if we [ ] (to leave) right now? [ ]

d. [ ] it [ ] (to be) easier for you if I speak more slowly and clearly? [ ]

e. If Jen [ ] (to win) the lottery, what would she do? [ ]

Grammar feed

First Conditional vs. Second Conditional

The choice depends on the probability of the situation:

First Conditional → possible future results
If I **pass** all my exams, I **will change** schools next year.

Second Conditional → hypothetical situation
If I **could** travel through time, I **would have** lots of fun.

5 **Listen to some teenagers talking about what they would do if they were city mayors. Then check (✓) the items they mention.**

42

a. Invest in the healthcare system [ ]

b. Develop flying cars [ ]

c. Shorten the school year [ ]

d. Reduce food consumption [ ]

e. Combat cyber bullying [ ]

f. Provide more delicious food at school [ ]

6 **Listen again. Complete these three other items mentioned by the teenagers.**

43

a. If I were the mayor, I [ ] guards in front of schools to help children cross the streets.

b. I [ ] the cycling conditions in the city.

c. If I were the mayor, all restaurants and supermarkets [ ] pet-friendly.

DOWNLOADING

7 **How about you? What would you do if you were the mayor of your town? Write four sentences using the Second Conditional.**

[ ]

[ ]

[ ]

[ ]

Your turn!

Now work with a partner. Take turns sharing your answers to Activity 7. Compare and contrast your views.

LOADING

1 **Laura and Kevin are talking about their new neighbors. Listen and read.**

44

Laura: Hey, Kev! You've met our new next-door neighbor, haven't you?

Kevin: No, not yet. Have you?

Laura: Yeah, I've just met her. Her name is Sheila. And guess what? Megan Rogers is her niece.

Kevin: Megan Rogers... She's an actress, isn't she?

Laura: Yes, exactly!

Kevin: The critics didn't like her last movie, did they?

Laura: No, they didn't. Do you know why?

Kevin: No, I don't. I actually liked it. It was a great thriller. You haven't seen it, have you?

Laura: No, not yet. Her aunt just told me. She was going through some personal problems and couldn't focus on her acting.

Kevin: Oh, that's too bad.

Laura: We all have problems, don't we– even famous people! Well, I'm going to her aunt's house to welcome her to the neighborhood. You'll come with me, won't you?

Kevin: Sure! I'm free now.

2 **Read the dialogue again and check (✓) the true sentence(s).**

a. Megan Rogers' last movie was a thriller. ☐

b. Both Laura and Kevin thought Megan Rogers' last movie was great. ☐

c. Both Laura and Kevin are going to visit their new neighbor. ☐

3 **Listen again and repeat the dialogue.**

45

Grammar feed

Tag Questions

Affirmative sentence → Negative tag	Negative sentence → Affirmative tag
You've met our new next-door neighbors, **haven't you**?	**The critics didn't** like her last movie, **did they**?
She's an actress, **isn't she**?	**You haven't** seen it, **have you**?
You'll come with me, **won't you**?	

UPLOADING

4 Match the sentences with the tag questions.

a. You like cycling,

b. Bruna Mayers is running for mayor,

c. Marlon didn't make it to work today,

d. You can skateboard,

e. Daniela hasn't broken her leg,

f. You're going to hitchhike,

g. The Rogers will move to a new house,

h. Kevin isn't Megan's friend,

☐	aren't you?	☐	did he?	☐	has she?	a	don't you?
☐	isn't she?	☐	is he?	☐	won't they?	☐	can't you?

5 Complete the sentences. Use the appropriate tag questions.

a. A city governor has many duties, doesn't he/she?

b. You commute to work by bike, ________?

c. Emily doesn't drive very carefully, ________?

d. You haven't been to Canada, ________?

e. He had called before you arrived, ________?

f. We had English class yesterday, ________?

g. The assistant position is available, ________?

DOWNLOADING

6 Write three statements about the challenges in a city like yours. Then write question tags for these statements.

____

____

____

Our city could be better connected and more productive, couldn't it?

Your turn!

Now work with a partner. Take turns asking and answering the questions in Activity 6. Pay attention to your intonation. If you think you know the answer, use downward intonation ↓. If you are not sure, use upward intonation ↑.

iSkills

iRead

1 What are the effects of car pollutants on the environment? Exchange ideas with your teacher and classmates.

2 Read the news headlines below. What are they talking about?

READING STRATEGY

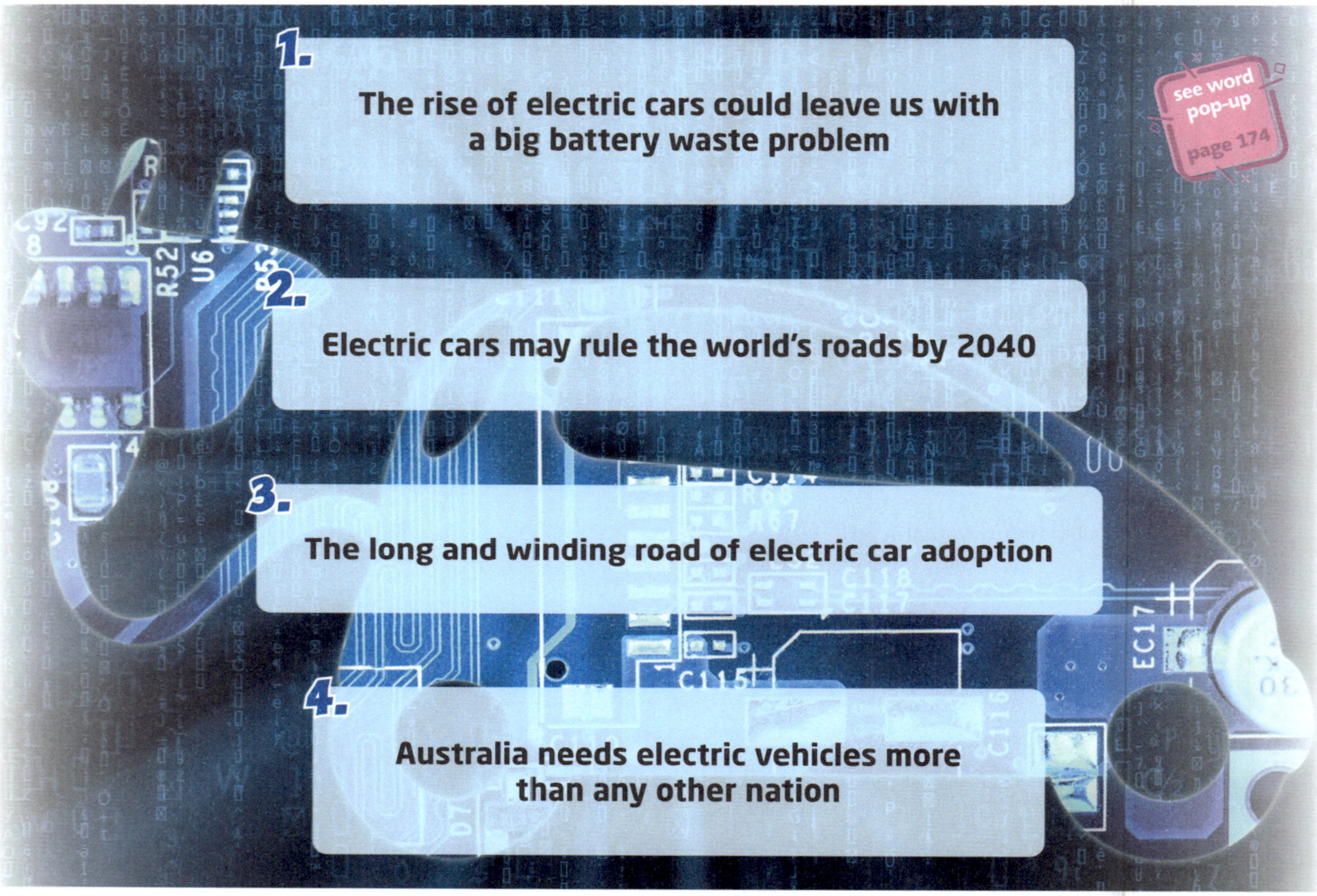

1. The rise of electric cars could leave us with a big battery waste problem

2. Electric cars may rule the world's roads by 2040

3. The long and winding road of electric car adoption

4. Australia needs electric vehicles more than any other nation

see word pop-up page 174

3 **The extracts below are part of the news of two of the headlines. Which ones? Check (✓) the correct box.**

"[...] while electric vehicle batteries might be taken to recycling facilities, there's no guarantee the lithium itself will be recovered if it doesn't pay to do so."

- [ ] headline 1
- [ ] headline 2
- [ ] headline 3
- [ ] headline 4

"Australia is now heading towards 100 per cent import dependency on fuel, primarily from the Middle East and through Asia."

- [ ] headline 1
- [ ] headline 2
- [ ] headline 3
- [ ] headline 4

English for • *Social Studies*

1 **What are green cities? How do cities become green? How green is your city? Are there many green cities in your country? What do you know about them? Share your views with your teacher and classmates.**

2 **Read the text and answer the questions.**

iThink

a. Are the three cities in the same country and continent?

b. What do they have in common?

THESE METROPOLISES AREN'T LITERALLY THE GREENEST PLACES ON EARTH, BUT THEY DESERVE RECOGNITION FOR HELPING THEIR RESIDENTS LIVE BETTER, GREENER LIVES.

Reykjavik, Iceland

Are you familiar with the saying "Greenland is icy and Iceland is green"? It's actually quite accurate, especially with the advancements that Iceland and its capital city, Reykjavik, have made in recent years. Reykjavik has incorporated hydrogen buses into its transportation system. The city's energy is also sourced from renewable geothermal and hydropower resources like the rest of Iceland. The city has set a goal to eliminate the use of fossil fuels by 2050, and the mayor is committed to making Reykjavik the most environmentally friendly city in Europe.

Portland, Oregon, U.S.

Portland stands out as one of the greenest places to live because of its unique approach to urban planning and outdoor spaces. As the first U.S. city to implement a comprehensive plan aimed at reducing CO2 emissions, it has built an impressive system of light rail, buses, and bike lanes to reduce reliance on cars. Additionally, it boasts 92,000 acres of green spaces and over 74 miles of hiking, running, and biking trails, making it an attractive location for outdoor enthusiasts.

Curitiba, Brazil

Curitiba's bus system is widely regarded as one of the best in the world, making the city a model for other urban areas. In addition, the city has municipal parks and preserved green spaces, with each resident having access to over 580 square feet of greenery. With about three-quarters of the population relying on public transportation, it's no surprise that 99 percent of Curitiba residents express satisfaction with their hometown according to one survey.

3 **Circle the correct alternative according to the text.**

see word pop-up page 174

project

a. Reykjavik is **the only city/one of the cities** in Iceland that uses heat and electricity from renewable geothermal and hydropower sources.

b. Portland **has/does not have** many miles of hiking, running, and biking trails.

c. Public transportation in Curitiba is so efficient that about **three-quarters/two-quarters** of its residents use it.

rePlay

1 **Work in small groups. Write a consequence chain story. Follow your teacher's instructions.**

Student A: If you arrived here earlier, you would meet Carlos.

Student B: If you met Carlos, you would probably become friends.

Student C: If you became friends, you would play soccer together.

2 **Work in pairs. Talk about what you would do in each of these scenarios.**

- If I won 1 million dollars, I would…
- If I could fly anywhere in the world, I would…
- If I had one day left to live, I would…
- If I could meet any famous person, I would…

3 **Play *Finish My Sentence*.**

If I lived in Australia, ...

... I would see koalas all the time.

Self-Assessment

Circle the correct option to complete the sentences.

1. What **would/did** you do if you were the coach of your soccer team?
2. If she **were/would be** the mayor, she **invested/would invest** in campaigns to encourage people to take part in community projects such as selling used goods to raise money for local charities.
3. If I weren't allergic to cats and dogs, I **did/would do** volunteer work in an animal shelter.
4. Life **would be/were** much better if there was less violence.
5. What would you do if your son **played/would play** the guitar in the middle of the night?
6. **Would/Will** you be afraid if aliens visited our planet?
7. Giovanna didn't come to school today, **does/did** she?
8. He had called before he arrived, **hadn't/didn't** he?
9. His position is still available, isn't **there/it**?
10. They had a math test last week, **didn't/hadn't** they?

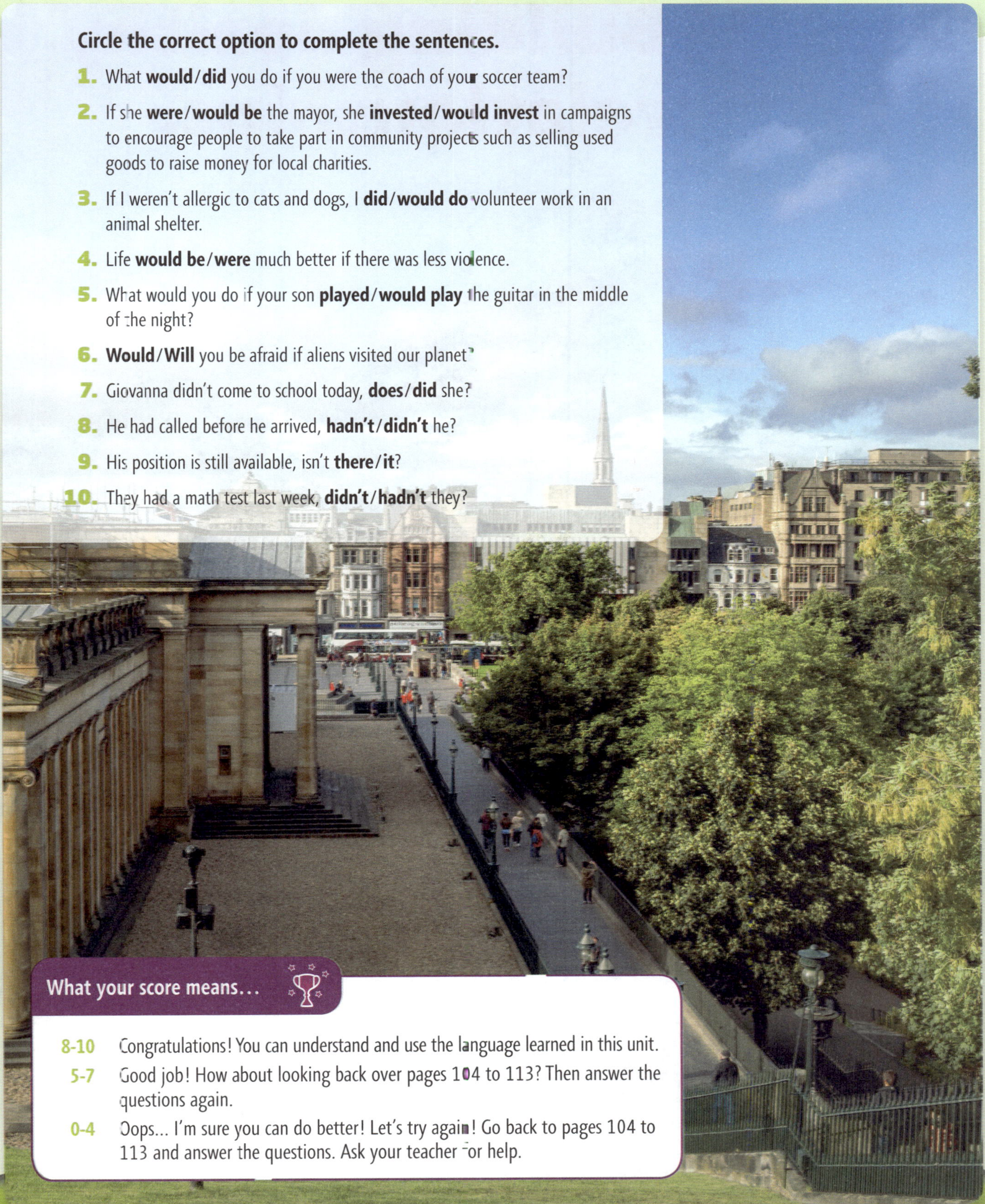

What your score means…

- **8-10** Congratulations! You can understand and use the language learned in this unit.
- **5-7** Good job! How about looking back over pages 104 to 113? Then answer the questions again.
- **0-4** Oops... I'm sure you can do better! Let's try again! Go back to pages 104 to 113 and answer the questions. Ask your teacher for help.

unit

8 Building healthy relationships.

» IN THIS UNIT YOU WILL

- learn how to say more about people and things using relative clauses
- learn how to refer back to people, places, and things using *something*, *someone/somebody*, and *somewhere*.
- review different ways of talking about the future

START UP

Let's plug in! Describe the picture. What is the relationship between the people in the picture? How important is it to build up relationships at different levels?

LOADING

1 Listen and read the quotes.

46

a. "Communication will bring understanding and understanding will cause harmonious mutual relationships **which** can establish peace and stability."
Lobsang Tenzin, Tibetan leader

b. "I do come from a very close family. And I'm fascinated, in particular, with family relationships and the relationships **that** we all form with friends who feel as close, if not closer, than family."
John Corey Whaley, American writer

c. "A true friend is someone **who** is there for you when he'd rather be anywhere else."
Len Wein, American cartoonist

d. "Friendship is something **that** creates equality and mutuality, not a reward for finding equality or a way of intensifying existing mutuality."
Rowan Williams, English theologian

e. "[...] And the person **who** was just a friend is suddenly the only person you can ever imagine yourself with."
Gillian Anderson, American actress and producer

f. "In my early professional years I was asking the question: How can I treat, or cure, or change this person? Now I would phrase the question in this way: How can I provide a relationship **which** this person may use for his own personal growth?"
Carl Rogers, American psychologist

2 Read the quotes again and underline the correct statement(s).

a. According to John Corey Whaley, family relationships are the most intimate we can have.
b. Carl Rogers believed that relationships could be used for our personal growth.
c. From Gillian Anderson's point of view, your friend can never become your romantic partner.
d. Lobsang Tenzin thought that communication was important for relationships.

Grammar feed

Relative Clauses

People → "A true friend is someone **who** is there for you when he'd rather be anywhere else."
"[...] And the person **who** was just a friend is suddenly the only person you can ever imagine yourself with."

Things → "Communication will bring understanding and understanding will cause harmonious mutual relationships **which** can establish peace and stability."
"[...] How can I provide a relationship **which** this person may use for his own personal growth?"

In these sentences, the relative pronouns **who** and **which** can be replaced by the relative pronoun **that**.

UPLOADING

3 **Look at some quotes from Activity 1 again and pay attention to the words in bold. What do they refer to? Underline the word(s) in the quote.**

a. "Communication will bring understanding and understanding will cause harmonious mutual relationships **which** can establish peace and stability."

b. "A true friend is someone **who** is there for you when he'd rather be anywhere else."

c. "Friendship is something **that** creates equality and mutuality, not a reward for finding equality or a way of intensifying existing mutuality."

4 **Use *who* or *which* to complete the quotes below.**

a. "I don't need a friend _____ changes when I change and _____ nods when I nod; my shadow does that much better."

Plutarch, Greek philosopher

b. "And now you are and I am and we're a mystery _____ will never happen again."

E. E. Cummings, American poet

c. "A real friend is one _____ walks in when the rest of the world walks out."

Walter Winchell, American journalist

d. "Share your weaknesses. Share your hard moments. Share your real side. It'll either scare away every fake person in your life or it will inspire them to finally let go of that mirage called "perfection," _____ will open the doors to the most important relationships you'll ever be a part of."

Dan Pearce, American writer

DOWNLOADING

5 **Finish these sentences to create your own quotes.**

a. The gift of friendship is something which _____.

b. Our parents are the people who _____.

c. My real friends are the ones who _____.

Your turn!

Work in groups of four. Share your quotes.

Which one is

- the most philosophical?
- the most interesting?
- the most touching?

LOADING

1 Lexi and Chris are reading an article about a very common type of relationship: the one we have with our neighbors. Listen, read, and complete the text.

47

READING STRATEGY

Neighborhoods have changed over the years.

In the past, people brought baskets of sandwiches or fruits to the new people on the block. Sometimes they offered to help with a project. A neighborhood representative would stop by for coffee and leave a list of important numbers. Neighbors shared tools and garden equipment so not everyone would need to go out and buy expensive items ________ they wouldn't use often.

Even today, all neighborhoods have their own personalities. Some tend to be more open to street parties and socializing, while others are made up of people ________ prefer to keep to themselves. The second group isn't bad; it's just not as warm and inviting. Many of them may have demanding jobs and other responsibilities, so they don't have time to socialize with their neighbors.

It doesn't matter the type of neighborhood you live in, there are still some basic etiquette rules you should follow to be a good neighbor. It's important to live in peace and harmony, and even though that's not always possible, you can at least do whatever it takes to prevent hostilities and long-lasting hard feelings. [...]

see word pop-up page 178

2 Read the text again. Then copy the parts of the sentences that rephrase the statements below.

a. Having a good relationship with your neighbors is important.

____

b. New neighbors were welcomed by friendly people who lived nearby.

____

c. Because some neighbors lead very busy lives, participating in social events is difficult.

____

____

Grammar feed

Relative Clauses

In Relative Clauses the Relative Pronouns can be used

- **as the subject:**
  "Some tend to be more open to street parties and socializing, while others are made up of people **who/that** prefer to stay to themselves."
- **as the object:**
  Neighbors shared tools and garden equipment so not everyone would need to go out and buy expensive items **which/that** they wouldn't use often."

Study this

Omission of Relative Pronouns

When the relative pronoun is the **object** of the relative clause, it can be omitted:

"[...] there are still some basic etiquette rules you should follow to be a good neighbor."

=

"[...] there are still some basic etiquette rules **which/that** you should follow to be a good neighbor."

UPLOADING

3 Choose the correct alternative to complete the sentences.

a. Do you know the man [who/that] married Elizabeth, the math teacher?

☐ which / that ☑ who / that ☐ ø

b. Being able to trust my family and friends was really the most important thing [ ] I learned.

☐ who / that / ø ☐ ø / that ☐ which / who

c. Friendship is an essential part of life [ ] teaches you to trust and love people.

☐ which / that ☐ ø / that ☐ ø / who

d. Anna is the woman [ ] I lived with during my childhood. She was like a mom to me.

☐ ø / which / that ☐ ø / who / that ☐ which / that

4 Join each pair of sentences using a relative pronoun. Write all the possible combinations, including omission (ø).

a. The woman waved us goodbye. She is our new next-door neighbor.

The woman who waved us goodbye is our new next-door neighbor.

b. There's a student in my classroom. He is South African.

c. On Tuesday I watched a movie. It was a love story.

d. Where's the essay? I gave it to you last class.

DOWNLOADING

5 The following words are related to relationships. Write definitions for them using relative clauses.

a. a classmate: A classmate is someone who studies with you.

b. community workers

c. affinity

d. politeness

Your turn!

Work with a partner. Take turns sharing your definitions from Activity 5.

LOADING

1 **Listen and read the conversation.**

48

2 **Read the conversation again. Then answer the questions.**

a. Why are the students throwing a farewell party?

b. Will Lily and her friends miss Ms. Brito?

c. When is she going to come back?

d. In Lily's mom's opinion, how will Ms. Brito react to the farewell party?

3 **Listen again and repeat the conversation.**

49

4 **Read the text again. Circle the verb structures used to talk about the future.**

Grammar feed

***Be Going to* vs. *Will* (Review)**

She**'s going to study** at Stanford University for 2 years!

But she**'s going to come back** in time for our graduation.

→ present intention, certainty, or plan

We **will miss** her a lot.

I**'ll go** now.

→ prediction or promise

→ decision made at the moment of speaking

UPLOADING

5 **Read these dialogues between people talking about their future. Then look at the bold words and check (✓) the best answer according to what they indicate.**

a.

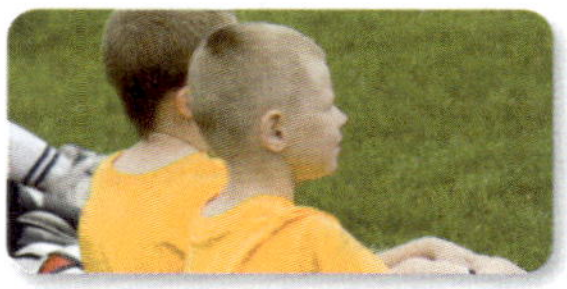

A: We **will win** this game!

B: I'm not so sure...

☐ a plan

☐ a prediction

b.

A: I'**ll** do my best to make you happy.

B: We both will.

☐ a promise

☐ a prediction

c.

A: Have you decided where you'**re going to study**?

B: Not yet, Dad. I'm still researching colleges.

☐ an intention or plan

☐ a decision made at the moment of speaking

d.

A: Who **are we going to play** against next Sunday?

B: St. Paul's team. The game is going to start at 4 p.m. Don't be late.

☐ a prediction

☐ certainty or plan

6 **Read the cartoon below. Why did Calvin and his mother use *will/won't* in their conversation?**

see word pop-up page 178

DOWNLOADING

7 **Creating and maintaining healthy relationships can be difficult. Complete the checklist with promises you will keep to make sure your relationships work well.**

From now on, for my relationships to be successful I will…

a. practice acceptance and gratitude

b. ______________________

c. ______________________

LOADING

1 **Ms. Amelia Brito is getting ready for her two-year stay at Stanford University. She is going to travel in 3 days. She's worried about her trip. Listen and read her conversation with Joel, her brother.**

50

Amelia: Can you believe I'm traveling in three days?

Joel: I know! These last weeks have gone so fast. Is everything ready?

Amelia: Pretty much everything, but I'm still nervous.

Joel: I wouldn't worry so much. I'm sure you'll make new friends easily.

Amelia: Yeah, I know that. Besides, as I'm traveling with two other friends, I'm sure I'll have some company there from the beginning.

Joel: Aren't you anxious about the professors you're going to have at Stanford University?

Amelia: I am! Relationships in the academic field can be hard. We are going to study there and work part time in an elementary school. So I hope I won't have problems bonding with my new students.

Joel: You'll do just fine. I have no doubts about it.

Amelia: I hope so. But now let me call the girls, because we're going out for a coffee this afternoon.

Joel: Ok. Have fun and let me know if you need any help.

2 **Read the dialogue again and write T (true) or F (false). Then correct the false statements.**

a. Amelia and Joel are traveling to Stanford in three days. F

Amelia and her two other friends are traveling to Stanford in three days.

b. Amelia is relaxed about her trip.

c. Joel is really worried about the relationships his sister will need to build.

d. Amelia isn't going to work as a teacher anymore.

e. Joel believes Amelia will do well at Stanford University.

3 **Listen again and repeat the dialogue.**

51

UPLOADING

4 **Read the text again. Find two examples of the Present Continuous used for arrangements. Write them on the lines below.**

____

____

Grammar feed

Present Continuous: future arrangements

We can also use the Present Continuous to talk about arrangements or plans previously organized for the future.

Can you believe I**'m traveling** in 3 days?

But now let me call the girls because we**'re going** out for a coffee this afternoon.

5 **Match the arrangements with how they were organized.**

a. The employees are meeting their boss this afternoon.
b. Lucia is flying to Rome to meet her fiancé.
c. We're having dinner at that fancy restaurant tonight.
d. Dad's working late tomorrow.
e. I'm going to the dentist on Monday morning.
f. The students are having a farewell party.

[ ] We have reservations for 9.
[ ] They've invited all their teachers.
[a] They have arranged to talk at 3:30 p.m.
[ ] He has a lot of work to catch up on.
[ ] They're going to get married there!
[ ] I have already called the secretary and scheduled an appointment.

6 **Write *Yes/No* questions or *Wh-* questions to find out about a friend's future arrangements.**

a. Are you doing anything interesting tonight? / What are you doing tonight?
b. ______________________________
c. ______________________________
d. ______________________________
e. ______________________________

DOWNLOADING

7 **Work with a partner. Ask him/her the questions from Activity 6. If your partner answers affirmatively, take notes on what he/she is doing.**

a. Yes, I am. I'm saying goodbye to a friend who is moving to Peru.
b. ______________________________
c. ______________________________
d. ______________________________
e. ______________________________

Your turn!

Share your partner's answers with the whole class.

She is saying goodbye to a friend who is moving to Peru.

iSkills

iListen

1 **Listen and read an interview with a YouTuber. Complete the questions the interviewer asked him.**

LEARNING STRATEGY

52

Interviewer: ______________________?
Why do you think this medium is best for your message?

YouTuber: I started making videos back in 2007, as a way to keep in touch with people while I was away at college. It was perfect for me because I could talk into a camera, show things around my dorm room, and introduce my high school friends and family to my college friends. Nearly a decade later, I could never have imagined it would turn into what it is now.

Interviewer: You share so much of yourself with your fans. ______________________?

YouTuber: There's PLENTY they don't know about me! Being in charge of what I share is something I really have to remember and be conscious of while creating, and making sure some things are just for me is so important. And if I told you, then it wouldn't be for just me, would it?

Interviewer: As a kid, ______________________?

YouTuber: I always thought I'd be a teacher! In fact, I went to school for it at Michigan State University, but it never ended up coming to fruition. In a way, YouTubers are kind of teachers. We have an opportunity to use our platform to share what we know with the world, and maybe get people to think a different way or see a different perspective.

Interviewer: ______________________?

YouTuber: A friend, an iPhone charger, and a pair of sweatpants.

2 **Listen again. Check (✓) the statements which are true.**

53

- [ ] He started making videos in 2006.
- [ ] He made videos to keep in touch with his family and friends.
- [ ] He always shares everything with his fans.
- [ ] When he was a child, he wanted to be a teacher.

iSpeak

3 **Work with a partner. Write two more questions you would like to ask a YouTuber. Then share your ideas with other classmates. Are there any similar questions?**

____

____

1 Have you ever been to a museum or an art gallery? If so, what did you see there? If not, would you like to go to a museum? What would you like to see there? What do you think we should look for when looking at a work of art? Share your ideas with your teacher and classmates.

iThink

2 Look at these two paintings.

Untitled, Jean-Michel Basquiat

MOIA's NYC Women's Cabinet, Aliza Nisenbaum

project

3 In groups, describe the paintings using relative clauses. Write some of your classmates sentences.

The first painting shows a man who has large feet.

rePlay

1 Play *The Never Ending Sentence* game.

2 Work in groups of four. Follow the instructions.

- Make a list of things or people and cut them up into little pieces.
- Put them in an envelope.
- One student chooses a piece of paper at random and keeps it secret.
- He or she gives clues about it, using a relative clause.

The other three people on the team get to guess what or who it is. The person who gets it correctly keeps the piece of paper and gets one point. Then, he/she chooses another piece of paper and gives clues.

Self-Assessment

Circle the correct option to complete the sentences.

1. Mr. Brown, **who/which** is a taxi driver, lives on the corner.
2. Do you know the girl **which/that** is sitting next to Bernardo?
3. I don't know **which/who** road I have to take.
4. Vincent Van Gogh is the artist **which/who** painted *Sunflowers*.
5. "A friend is the one **who/ø** comes in when the whole world has gone out." – Grace Pulpit
6. "I don't need a friend **ø/who** changes when I change and **ø/who** nods when I nod; my shadow does that much better." – Plutarch
7. London is a city **which/ø** has more modern buildings than ancient castles.
8. Her children **study/are going to study** in Canada for one year.
9. Oh, I'm late. **I'll leave/'m going to leave** right now. Otherwise I won't get there in time to catch the bus.
10. The students **are having/will have** a farewell party on Saturday evening. They have already arranged everything.

What your score means...

8-10	Congratulations! You can understand and use the language learned in this unit.
5-7	Good job! How about looking back over pages 118 to 127? Then answer the questions again.
0-4	Oops... I'm sure you can do better! Let's try again! Go back to pages 118 to 127 and answer the questions. Ask your teacher for help.

Rewind 4 Units 7 - 8

1 Answer the questions using the prompts given and the First or the Second Conditional. Write full answers.

a. What will you do if you don't get a good grade in math? (to go to extra classes)

If I don't get a good grade in math, I'll go to extra classes.

b. What would you do if you were the mayor of your town? (to listen to the citizens' requests)

If I were the mayor of my town, I would listen to the citizens' requests.

c. What would you do if you had a lot of money? (to do volunteer work around the world)

d. What would you do if you found some money on the street? (to take it to the nearest police station)

e. What will you do if you miss this bus? (to wait for the next one)

f. What will you do if your stomachache gets worse? (to see a doctor)

2 Match the columns.

a. His government has been successful,			aren't we?
b. Urban transport and mobility were not mentioned,			hasn't it?
c. We're now facing the same problems as big cities,			shouldn't they?
d. The International Conference on Urban Transportation and the Environment started in 1995,			were they?
e. Downtown bike lanes in Toronto should be permanent,			didn't it?

3 Complete the following texts with *who* or *which*.

a. Teens ______ feel confident and accepted may also be less likely to engage in the bullying of others.

b. Being a good role model is important too. Parents ______ like to spend time with their own friends are more likely to have children with lots of healthy friendships.

c. Loyalty and friendship, ______ are the same to me, created all the wealth that I've ever thought I'd have.

4 Read the fable. Then order the events.

The Lion and the Mouse

Once, when a Lion was sleeping, a little Mouse started running up and down on him; suddenly, the Lion woke up. He placed his huge paw on him, and opened his big jaws to swallow him. "I'm sorry", cried the little Mouse. "Please let me go and I promise I will repay you one day". The Lion found the idea of the Mouse being able to help him so amusing that he let him go. Some time after, the Lion was caught in a trap, and the hunters, who wanted to carry him alive to the King, tied him to a tree while they looked for a wagon to carry him on. The Mouse heard the Lion's roar. He followed the loud roar and saw the sad and unfortunate situation in which the Lion was. The mouse went up to him and soon chewed the ropes that bound the King of the Beasts. "See? I was right", said the little Mouse.

- [ ] The lion caught the mouse.
- [ ] The lion woke up.
- [ ] The lion was caught in a trap.
- [ ] The lion was sleeping.
- [ ] The mouse saved the lion.
- [ ] The mouse convinced the lion not to kill him.

5 What is the moral of the story? Check (✓).

- [ ] Never trust your enemy.
- [ ] Don't underestimate people.
- [ ] Everyone is our friend.

6 Answer these questions about you. Use true information.

a. What are you doing after class?

____

b. Where are you spending New Year's Eve this year?

____

c. Who are you having dinner with tomorrow evening?

____

READING HUB

Reading Hub

1 Do you find it hard to make new friends? Why?

2 Read about the benefits of friendships.

How to Make Good Friends

Meeting People and Making Meaningful Connections

The presence of strong friendships can significantly influence your well-being and happiness. Supportive friends reduce stress, provide comfort, prevent loneliness, and can even enhance your physical well-being. However, forming close friendships requires effort. It can be challenging for many of us to meet new people and establish meaningful relationships. But regardless of your age, it's always possible to forge new friendships, reconnect with old ones, and enhance your social life, emotional well-being, and overall health.

Why are friendships so important?

Romantic relationships receive a lot of emphasis in our society with the belief that finding the perfect partner will bring us happiness. However, studies indicate that our psychological well-being is actually influenced more by friendships. Research shows that friends contribute more to our happiness than any other factor.

The benefits of having friends

Developing and maintaining friendships requires time and effort, but having good friends can have various benefits:

- **Boost your mood.** Spending time with happy and positive friends can lift your mood and improve your outlook on life.
- **Assist you in achieving your goals.** Whether you›re working on getting in shape, quitting smoking, or making other improvements, the support and encouragement of a friend can significantly enhance your determination and increase your likelihood of success.
- **Alleviate your stress and depression.** Maintaining an active social life can boost your immune system and decrease feelings of isolation, a major contributor to depression.
- **Provide support during challenging times.** Even just having someone to confide in can help you navigate serious illness, job loss, the loss of a loved one, the end of a relationship, or other life challenges.
- **Offer support as you age.** As we age, retirement, illness, and the loss of loved ones can lead to feelings of isolation. Having reliable people in your life can give you a sense of purpose as you age and serve as a buffer against depression, disability, and loss.
- **Enhance your sense of self-worth.** Friendship is a give-and-take relationship. Being there for your friends can make you feel valued and give meaning to your life.

3 Read the text again and write YES or NO.

a. Research shows that friendship is even more important than romantic relationships. ☐

b. People can make new friends whatever their age. ☐

c. Friendships do not bring any benefits to our lives. ☐

see word pop-up page 150

1 What is a meme? What are some characteristics of memes that go viral? Answers will vary.

2 Read two memes about doing chores. Then mark the sentences T (true) or F (false).

a.

b.

a) The person who created meme A probably feels happy when they finish cleaning the house. [ ]

b) The person who made meme B is probably an adult who lives with their children. [ ]

3 Write a meme for the picture below.

Answers will vary.

1 What are the positive effects of social media? Do most young people use social media correctly? Why/Why not? Share your ideas with your teacher and classmates.

2 Read the following blog post and check if you mentioned any of the benefits the author mentions in her text.

The good side of social media

Social media is an integral part of today's society. The people who are at the forefront of molding the future of social networking sites are teens and children. This is because vast majority of the people who use the Internet are children and teens. Reportedly, many teens spend an average of 8 hours online every day. Much of that time is thought to be spent on social media sites, with only some attention focused on research and learning.

For the past decade, social media has been touted as a platform for youngsters to congregate online and interact socially as if they were in person, regardless of their distance from each other. There are likely teens out there who do not know of many other uses of the Internet other than their favorite social media platform.

While there have been many negative outcomes of social media such as cyberbullying and other online dangers, social media can be used in ways that promote positive and productive ideas in society. These positive behaviors make social media an invaluable tool for young people if used correctly.

Here are some of the ways in which social media can be used to benefit young people:

1. Social media can be used to educate young people.
2. Social media can be used as a voice of reason in society.
3. Social media has enabled more young people to be creative and innovative.
4. Social media has given teens the ability to hone different skills that are important in the real world.
5. Social media gives teens skills to become more confident and independent.

3 Correct the mistakes in each sentence.

see word pop-up page 150

a. It is said that many teens spend ~~at least~~ 8 hours online every day.

an average of

b. Teenagers spend most of their time on research and learning.

c. Most teens know different uses of Internet.

d. Social media hasn't helped more young people to be creative and innovative.

1 What is important to older people nowadays? Are older people similar all over the world? Explain. Exchange ideas with your teacher and classmates.

2 Read the infographic below. How are they similar to older people in Brazil?

WHAT MATTERS MOST TO OLDER ADULTS TODAY

Health & Wellness
Physical Health: Regular check-ups, exercise, healthy diet.
Mental Health: Stress management, mental stimulation, social connections.

Financial Security
Retirement Savings: Adequate funds for comfort and emergencies.
Pension & Benefits: Understanding and maximizing entitlements.

Family & Relationships
Family Time: Spending quality moments with loved ones.
Social Interaction: Maintaining friendships and community ties.

Independence & Autonomy
Living Arrangements: Safe, accessible homes or suitable senior living options.
Daily Activities: Ability to perform daily tasks independently.

Technology & Connectivity
Digital Literacy: Staying updated with technology for communication and convenience.
Online Services: Using the internet for shopping, healthcare, and socializing.

Lifelong Learning & Engagement
Education: Pursuing new skills or hobbies.
Community Involvement: Volunteering or participating in local events.

Safety & Security
Home Safety: Installing safety measures to prevent accidents.
Emergency Preparedness: Having plans and contacts for urgent situations.

Quality of Life
Comfort & Enjoyment: Access to leisure activities, travel, and personal fulfillment.
Respect & Dignity: Being valued and heard in all aspects of life.

3 **Match the examples to the categories. Write the letters.**

a. Health and Wellness b. Family and relationships c. Safety and security d. Lifelong learning

1. annual check-ups ☐ **2.** learning to knit and sew ☐ **3.** safety rails and emergency contact lists ☐ **4.** spending weekends with grandchildren ☐

1 **Are teenagers' reading habits influenced by the Internet? How? Do you think people your age read more print books or e-books? Exchange ideas with your teacher and classmates.**

2 **Read part of an article about teens and print books.**

YOUNG PEOPLE STILL PREFER PRINT TO E-BOOKS

Despite the rise of digital technology, many young people still prefer print books over e-books. Recent surveys reveal that printed books continue to hold a strong appeal among younger demographics, even in an era dominated by digital media.

According to a 2023 study, 60% of millennials and Gen Z respondents aged 18-29 indicated a preference for printed books over digital formats. This statistic is notable given that e-books and digital reading platforms are more accessible than ever before. The study found that 45% of young people read primarily in print, while only 25% reported reading e-books as their main format. The remaining 30% use a mix of both formats.

One reason for this preference is the tactile experience associated with print books. Many young readers indicated the physical feel of a book, including its texture and weight, as a key factor in their choice. Many also appreciate the aesthetic appeal of physical books, including cover art and the satisfaction of building a personal library.

Moreover, a 2022 report revealed that 55% of young readers find printed books easier on the eyes compared to screens, which can cause digital fatigue. Some specialists also noted that reading on screens can lead to eye strain and decreased focus over time.

Another factor contributing to the enduring popularity of printed books is the social and emotional value they attach to physical books. A 2024 survey found that 65% of respondents prefer to give and receive books as gifts, reflecting a cultural value placed on tangible, personal items. Printed books are often seen as meaningful and cherished possessions, which digital formats may not replicate.

3 **Read the following sentences in the article again. Then write *fact* or *opinion*.**

a. According to a 2023 study, 60% of millennials and Gen Z respondents aged 18-29 indicated a preference for printed books over digital formats. ______

b. Printed books are often seen as meaningful and cherished possessions, which digital formats may not replicate. ______

c. Moreover, a 2022 report revealed that 55% of young readers find printed books easier on the eyes compared to screens, which can cause digital fatigue ______

1 Is Brazil a good place for foreigners to live? Talk to a classmate and justify your answer.

2 Read a part of the survey about expats in Brazil and check the correct statement about it.

Your Country Through Expat Eyes

Country Report

Brazil

Life in Brazil

	2017*		2016*
Overall Rank	**62**	▲2	**64**
Quality of Life	62		62
Ease of Settling	33		33
Working Abroad	63	▲2	65
Family Life (out of 45 countries)	43	▲2	45
Personal Finance	54	▲5	59
Cost of Living	54		54
	*out of 65 countries		*out of 67 countries

68% generally satisfied

Expats in Brazil

Avarage age: **45.3** years

Gender split: **61%** male, **39%** female

Relationship status: **79%** in a relationship, **21%** single

Top nationalities

15% U.S. American

9% British

6% Portuguese

Working in Brazil

Avarage working hours: **44.4h** a week (full time)

Top field of work: **19%** education

Top income groups: **28%** 12-25k USD; **23%** 25k-50k USD; **28%** 100-150k USD

Top employment statuses: **13%** employee; **13%** looking for work; **13%** teacher/academic staff/researcher

Top Reasons for Relocating

#1 Moved for love **#2** Sent by employer **#3** Adventure/personal challenge

- [ ] There are more female than male expats in Brazil.
- [ ] Sports facilities are among the three main reasons for relocating.
- [ ] More than half of the expats are generally satisfied with their lives in Brazil.
- [ ] Expats in Brazil are mostly teenagers who are attending high school.

see word pop-up page 170

3 Read the text again and choose three facts that called your attention. Share your opinion with friends. Are they the same?

1 Are all cities good for urban cycling? Is investment in improving infrastructure for cyclists a modern and intelligent move for a city to make? What are the most bicycle-friendly cities in the world? Exchange ideas with your teacher and classmates.

2 Read the text and check if you mentioned any cities included in the Bicycle-Friendly Cities Index 2019.

The Copenhagenize Bicycle-Friendly Cities Index 2019

The announcement of the most extensive list and ranking of bicycle-friendly towns in the world, The Copenhagenize Index, is always something to look forward to. Since the launch of the biannual rating in 2011, this is the fifth Index (2019). Although the selection is a lengthy and difficult one, the process is undeniably motivating and thought-provoking. And one thing is certain: the results never fail to surprise.
The Copenhagenize Index changes biannually. There have been several changes made to the 2019 edition. Compared to 2011, they now have 600 cities registered in their database, a significant increase over the 80 they did in 2011. The data set continues to change as they occasionally add and remove cities. This year, they've added a new section called " Success Stories" where people share inspiring bike stories from different parts of the world, beyond the ones listed in the Top 20. These stories demonstrate the various ways in which bike friendships can come in many forms.

The Top 20 – 2019

1. Copenhagen
2. Amsterdam
3. Utrecht
4. Antwerp
5. Strasbourg
6. Bordeaux
7. Oslo
8. Paris
9. Vienna
10. Helsinki
11. Bremen
12. Bogotá
13. Barcelona
14. Ljubljana
15. Berlin
16. Tokyo
17. Taipei
18. Montréal
19. Vancouver
20. Hamburg

3 Underline the sentence that is false according to the text.

a. The number of cities ranked has increased from 80 in 2011 to 600 in 2019.

b. They added a new section about inspiring bike stories.

c. Amsterdam is at the top of the list in the most recent version.

see word pop-up page 174

1 **How often do you use a dictionary when you are studying English? What kind of dictionary do you use? What kind of information can you find in an English-English dictionary? Share your ideas with your teacher and classmates.**

2 **Look at the dictionary entries below and answer the questions that follow.**

friendship (noun): a relationship between friends.

friendless (adjective): having no friends and no one to help you.

relationship (noun): the way in which two people or two groups feel about each other and behave towards each other.

trust (noun/verb): a strong belief in the honesty, goodness, etc. of someone or something.

a. Which word is an adjective?

b. Define the word from the previous item with a relative pronoun.

c. Which word is both a verb and a noun?

d. In the sentence "I'm sure they trust you", is the word trust a noun or a verb?

e. Write a sentence for each of the entries.

Irregular verbs

Base form	Past form	Past Participle	Translation
awake	awoke	awaken	acordar
be	was, were	been	ser, estar
become	became	become	tornar-se
begin	began	begun	começar
bend	bent	bent	dobrar
bet	bet	bet	apostar
bite	bit	bitten	morder
blow	blew	blown	soprar
break	broke	broken	quebrar
bring	brought	brought	trazer
build	built	built	construir
burn	burnt/burned	burnt/burned	queimar
buy	bought	bought	comprar
catch	caught	caught	pegar
choose	chose	chosen	escolher
come	came	come	vir
cut	cut	cut	cortar
do	did	done	fazer
draw	drew	drawn	desenhar
dream	dreamed/dreamt	dreamed/dreamt	sonhar
drink	drank	drunk	beber
drive	drove	driven	dirigir
eat	ate	eaten	comer
fall	fell	fallen	cair
feed	fed	fed	alimentar
feel	felt	felt	sentir
fight	fought	fought	lutar
find	found	found	achar
fly	flew	flown	voar
forget	forgot	forgotten	esquecer
forgive	forgave	forgiven	perdoar
get	got	got/gotten	conseguir
get up	got up	got up/ gotten up	levantar-se
give	gave	given	dar
go	went	gone	ir
grow	grew	grown	crescer
hang out	hung out	hung out	passar tempo
have	had	had	ter
hear	heard	heard	ouvir
hide	hid	hidden	esconder
hit	hit	hit	atingir
hold	held	held	segurar
hurt	hurt	hurt	machucar
keep	kept	kept	manter

Base form	Past form	Past Participle	Translation
know	knew	known	saber, conhecer
lean	leant/leaned	leant/leaned	inclinar-se
learn	learnt/learned	learnt/learned	aprender
leave	left	left	deixar, sair
lend	lent	lent	emprestar
let	let	let	deixar
lose	lost	lost	perder
make	made	made	fazer
mean	meant	meant	significar
meet	met	met	encontrar
overcome	overcame	overcome	superar
pay	paid	paid	pagar
put	put	put	colocar
read	read	read	ler
ride	rode	ridden	andar de
ring	rang	rung	tocar
rise	rose	risen	subir, aumentar
run	ran	run	correr
say	said	said	dizer
see	saw	seen	ver
sell	sold	sold	vender
send	sent	sent	enviar
set	set	set	estabelecer
show	showed	shown	mostrar
sing	sang	sung	cantar
sit	sat	sat	sentar
sleep	slept	slept	dormir
speak	spoke	spoken	falar
spell	spelled/spelt	spelled/spelt	soletrar
spend	spent	spent	gastar, passar tempo
split	split	split	dividir
stand up	stood up	stood up	ficar de pé
steal	stole	stolen	roubar
swim	swam	swum	nadar
take	took	taken	pegar, tomar
teach	taught	taught	ensinar
tell	told	told	contar
think	thought	thought	pensar
throw	threw	thrown	jogar
understand	understood	understood	entender
wake up	woke up	waken up	acordar
wear	wore	worn	vestir
win	won	won	ganhar
write	wrote	written	escrever

WORKBOOK

WORKBOOK

Grammar Reference

SIMPLE PAST

A: What **did you** do this weekend?
B: I **played** video games and **ate** popcorn with Mia.
A: That sounds fun!

A: Did you travel to New York on your vacation?
B: No, I **didn't**. I **went** camping with my cousins.

Quando queremos expressar ações e estados iniciados e concluídos em um momento definido no passado, usamos o ***Simple Past***.
Formar esse tempo verbal é muito simples. Na afirmativa para verbos regulares, acrescentamos ***-ed*** ao final do verbo.
Na negativa, para todas as pessoas, usamos ***did not*** ou ***didn't*** e o verbo principal na ***base form*** (no infinitivo sem ***to***).
Para fazer perguntas no ***Simple Past***, usamos a seguinte estrutura: ***did* + sujeito + verbo na *base form***.

Importante:

- É preciso memorizar a forma dos verbos irregulares no ***Simple Past***. Em caso de dúvida, vale consultar uma lista com esses verbos (como a que aparece nas páginas 144 e 145 do livro).
- Quando usamos o auxiliar ***did*** em perguntas ou em frases negativas, o verbo volta para a ***base form***.
- Para formar ***wh- questions***, basta começar a pergunta com a ***wh- word*** (como ***what*** ou ***who***). O restante fica com a mesma estrutura das ***yes/no questions***.

Agora faça a atividade 1.

COMPARATIVES AND SUPERLATIVES

Cars are **more expensive** than bikes.

Trucks are **bigger** than cars and bikes.

Bikes are one of **the smallest** means of transportation.

Trucks are **the most useful** vehicles for people when they move house.

Comparative

small → small**er** than
useful → **more** useful than
expensive → **more** expensive than

Superlative

small → the small**est**
useful → the **most** useful
expensive → the **most** expensive

Exceptions: Comparative and Superlative

good → better than → the best
bad → worse than → the worst
far → farther/further than → the farthest/furthest

Utilizamos o ***comparative*** para comparar dois ou mais elementos.
O ***superlative***, por sua vez, indica o elemento que tem a característica mais marcada ou elevada dentro de um grupo.
Em inglês, o ***comparative*** e o ***superlative*** são formados de maneira semelhante.

Comparativo:

- com adjetivos de *uma sílaba*, adicionamos ***-er*** ao final da palavra, que é, na maioria das vezes, seguida de ***than***;
- com adjetivos de *duas ou mais sílabas*, usamos a seguinte estrutura: ***more* + *adjetivo* + *than***.

Superlativo:

- com adjetivos de *uma sílaba*, adicionamos ***-est*** ao final da palavra;
- com adjetivos de *duas ou mais sílabas*, usamos a seguinte estrutura: ***the most* + *adjetivo***.

Importante:

- Quando o adjetivo que tem apenas *uma sílaba* termina em ***consoante* + *vogal* + *consoante*** (CVC), dobramos a última consoante e acrescentamos ***-er*** para formar o ***comparative*** e ***-est*** para formar o ***superlative***.
- Em adjetivos de *uma sílaba* terminados em ***-e***, acrescentamos apenas ***-r*** para formar o ***comparativo*** e ***-st*** para formar o ***superlativo***.
- No caso de adjetivos de *duas sílabas* terminados em ***-y***, tiramos o ***-y*** e acrescentamos ***-ier*** para formar o comparativo e ***-iest*** para formar o superlativo.

Agora faça a atividade 2.

1 Complete the sentences with the Simple Past form of the verbs in parentheses.

J. K. Rowling

Born at Yate General Hospital, a short distance from Bristol, on July 31, 1965, Joanne Rowling spent (spend) her early years in Gloucestershire, England, and Chepstow, Gwent, South Wales.

Jo ______ (attend) Wyedean Comprehensive, where her mother, Anne, ______ (work) as a science technician in the Chemistry department, while her father, Peter, ______ (be) an aircraft engineer at the Rolls Royce facility in Bristol. Jo ______ (know) from a young age that she wanted to write. When she was six years old, she ______ (write) "Rabbit," a tale about a rabbit.

She ______ (relocate) to northern Portugal to teach English as a foreign language, carrying notebooks full of ideas for the Harry Potter series with her. In October 1992, she ______ (marry) Jorge Arantes and ______ (have) a daughter, Jessica in 1993.

Jo ______ (complete) her teacher training in Edinburgh and started working in the city's schools, but she never ______ (stop) writing in her own time.

Under the pen name J.K. Rowling, Bloomsbury Children's Books ______ (release) the first book in the Harry Potter series in June 1997.

2 Circle the correct form of comparative or superlative.

a. The sun is **bright/brighter** than the moon.

b. Oranges are **sweeter/the sweetest** than lemons.

c. Airplanes are **more expensive/fast** than helicopters.

d. The Nile is **longer/the longest** river in the world.

iCan

Check (✓) the box that best describes your performance in this unit.

1. I can describe and ask about events in the past.	☐ Yes, I can.	☐ Not sure.
2. I can describe and ask about actions in the past.	☐ Yes, I can.	☐ Not sure.
3. I can use the comparative of superiority.	☐ Yes, I can.	☐ Not sure.
4. I can use the superlative form.	☐ Yes, I can.	☐ Not sure.

ADVICE: *SHOULD* (REVIEW)

You **should** talk to your teacher about any issues related to bullying.

Para dar conselhos a alguém, empregamos, na afirmativa, o modal ***should***, seguido do verbo principal na ***base form***.

Na negativa, basta acrescentarmos ***not*** após ***should*** ou usarmos a forma contraída ***shouldn't***. Esse verbo tem a mesma forma para todas as pessoas.

Agora faça a atividade 1.

FORMAL OBLIGATIONS AND PROHIBITIONS: *MUST* AND *MUST NOT*

You **must** be silent in this area.
You **must not** use your cell phone in this area.

Na afirmativa, usamos ***must*** em situações formais para expressar uma obrigação. Esse verbo assume a mesma forma para todas as pessoas e é seguido sempre da ***base form*** do verbo principal.

Na negativa, acrescentamos ***not*** a esse modal ou empregamos a forma contraída ***mustn't***. Nesse contexto, o verbo expressa uma proibição.

Importante:

- Em situações menos formais, podemos empregar ***can't*** em vez de ***must not***.
- Na afirmativa, ***can*** indica que algo é possível, ao passo que ***must*** expressa uma obrigação.
- ***Have to***, assim como ***must***, indica uma obrigação. Contudo, ***don't/doesn't have to*** indica que algo não é obrigatório, ao passo que ***must not*** expressa que algo é proibido.

Agora faça as atividades 2, 3 e 4.

WILL VS. *MIGHT*

Kate: I hope you like your new school in Seattle, Dave. We **will** miss you!
Dave: Thanks, Kate! I **will** miss everybody, too.
Kate: **Will** you play in the school band there, too?
Dave: Sure, but I **might** play a new instrument.

Usamos ***will*** para falar sobre acontecimentos certos no futuro. Ele é seguido sempre da ***base form*** do verbo principal e assume a mesma forma para todas as pessoas do discurso.

Para formar a negativa com ***will***, acrescentamos ***not*** ao verbo ou usamos a forma contraída ***won't***.

Empregamos o verbo ***might*** seguido da ***base form*** do verbo principal, por sua vez, quando queremos expressar uma possibilidade, mas não uma certeza no futuro.

Importante:

- a negativa de ***might*** é ***might not***.

Agora faça a atividade 5.

DEGREES OF POSSIBILITY: MAY, COULD, AND MIGHT

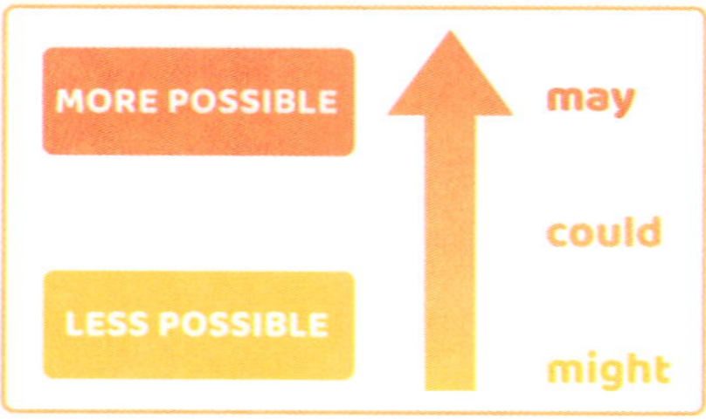

The bus **may** arrive soon.
The bus **could** arrive soon.
The bus **might** arrive soon.

Usamos ***may***, ***could*** e ***might*** para indicar a possiblidade de algo acontecer ou não. Esses verbos têm o sentido semelhante, mas expressam graus diferentes de certeza em relação às chances de algo se concretizar.

May indica que algo tem maior possibilidade de acontecer.

Could expressa a ideia de que algo pode acontecer, mas com menor grau de certeza do que a ação ou estado indicado por ***may***.

Might, por fim, indica que algo pouco provavelmente acontecerá.

Esses verbos têm a mesma forma para todas as pessoas do discurso e vêm seguidos do verbo principal na ***base form***.

Na negativa, basta acrescentar ***not*** após esses modais.

Importante:

- desses três verbos, apenas ***could*** tem uma forma contraída na negativa: ***couldn't***.

Agora faça as atividades 6 e 7.

Word pop-up

spreading – espalhando
bonds – elos, laços
exchanged – passado de *to exchange*, trocou
somehow – de alguma forma
to cope – lidar
maintenance – manutenção
roughly – por volta de
measuring – medir
device – aparelho
self-worth – autovalorização
to struggle – lutar
welfare – bem-estar

1 Look at the pictures. Then complete with *should* or *shouldn't* according to each situation.

a. They ________ spread rumors about other people.

d. Lynn ________ be rude to people.

b. He ________ give his seat to senior citizens.

e. You ________ turn the volume down.

c. People ________ talk loudly in the library.

f. You ________ clean the tray before leaving the cafeteria.

2 Look at this street sign and write T (true) or F (false).

On the first and third Tuesday of each month...

a. you can park on this side of the street in the afternoon. [T]

b. you must park on the other side of the street in the morning. [ ]

c. you must not park on this side of the street at 7 a.m. [ ]

d. you can park here anytime. [ ]

e. you must park your car on this side of the street in the morning. [ ]

3 Now look at the sign below and check (✓) the correct answers.

a. This is a sign for people who want to cross the street. ✓

b. This is a sign for people and cars. ☐

c. Pedestrians must push the button to cross the road. ☐

d. Pedestrians must not cross if walk signal is not shown. ☐

4 Read these pool rules and write sentences using *must* or *must not*.

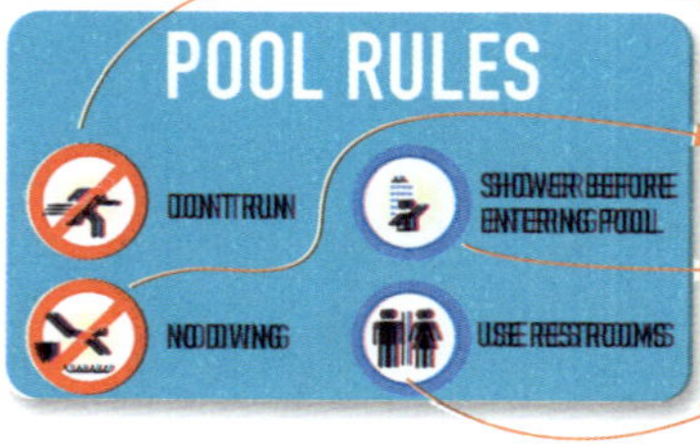

a. You must not run.

b. ______

c. ______

d. ______

5 Look at the pictures and complete the predictions.

a. He will be late.

d. The red team might ______.

b. The boy will ______.

e. The woman might ______.

c. She will ______.

f. The toast won't ______.

6 Look at the table. Check (✓) the correct column according to your plans. Then write sentences about them.

	I may...	I could...	I might...
a. travel abroad in 5 years' time			
b. move to another city/neighborhood next year			
c. get a new smartphone			
d. watch a movie next weekend			
e. learn a new language			
f. visit a friend next Saturday			

a. I may travel abroad in 5 years' time. My family is saving money for this trip.

b. ______

c. ______

d. ______

e. ______

f. ______

7 Match the columns to form sentences.

a. The baby is crying. [ ] My cousins may stay there.

b. It's already 3:00 p.m. [ ] It might be Mom calling us.

c. There are maps at the entrance of the zoo. [ ] We may get one so that we don't get lost.

d. The phone is ringing. [a] He might be hungry.

e. We have an extra room at our house. [ ] I'm sure we could be friends.

f. She's so nice and friendly. [ ] If we don't hurry we will be late for class.

iCan

Check (✓) the box that best describes your performance in this unit.

1. I can use *should* to give people advice. [ ] Yes, I can. [ ] Not sure.

2. I can talk about permission using *can*. [ ] Yes, I can. [ ] Not sure.

3. I can talk about obligations and prohibitions using *must (not)*. [ ] Yes, I can. [ ] Not sure.

4. I can discuss possibilities using *may*, *might*, *could*. [ ] Yes, I can. [ ] Not sure.

I've cleaned my room.

PRESENT PERFECT: EVENTS AT AN INDEFINITE TIME IN THE PAST

Miles **has finished** eating breakfast, but he **hasn't washed** the dishes.

Affirmative

Singular	**Plural**
I / You = have ('ve) He / She / It = has ('s)	We / You / They = have ('ve)

Negative

Singular	**Plural**
I / You = have not He / She / It = has not	We / You / They = have not

Contractions: haven't / hasn't

Em inglês, usamos o ***Present Perfect*** para falar sobre ações em um passado não definido.

Para formar esse tempo verbal, usamos ***have*** ou ***has*** (para a 3ª pessoa do singular) e o verbo principal no particípio passado (***Past Participle***).

Na negativa, acrescentamos ***not*** após ***have*** ou ***has*** ou empregamos as respectivas formas contraídas ***haven't*** ou ***hasn't***, mais comuns na fala e em contextos menos formais de comunicação.

Importante:

- Em caso de dúvidas sobre a forma ***Past Participle*** dos verbos irregulares, você pode consultar um dicionário ou a lista presente nas páginas 144 e 145.

Agora faça as atividades 1, 2, e 3.

SIMPLE PAST VS. PRESENT PERFECT

Anne and her sister **arrived** home this morning, but they **haven't unpacked**.

Tanto o ***Simple Past*** quanto o ***Present Perfect*** são usados para tratar de acontecimentos e estados no passado.

O ***Simple Past*** expressa ações já concluídas.

O ***Present Perfect***, por sua vez, indica que a ação ocorreu em um passado não definido ou uma ação que se iniciou, mas não foi concluída ainda. Não usamos expressões de tempo (como ***yesterday***) nesse tempo verbal.

Agora faça a atividade 4.

PRESENT PERFECT: *YES/NO* QUESTIONS

Harry: **Have you** ever **eaten** fish and chips?
Tom: Yes, **I have**. It's delicious!

Interrogative

Singular	**Plural**
Have I / you ...? **Has** he / she / it ...?	**Have** we / you / they ...?

Para formar ***yes/no questions*** no ***Present Perfect***, seguimos a estrutura ***have*** ou ***has*** + sujeito + verbo principal no ***Past Participle***.

O advérbio ***ever*** é usado somente em perguntas no ***Present Perfect***. Ele pode ser traduzido como "já" e indica que queremos saber sobre toda a experiência da pessoa até o momento em que fazemos a pergunta. Ele fica entre o sujeito e o verbo no ***Past Participle***.

Nas respostas a ***yes/no questions***, utilizamos, na maioria das vezes, apenas ***have*** ou ***has***, sem o verbo principal.

Agora faça as atividades 5 e 6.

PRESENT PERFECT WITH *ALREADY* AND *YET*

Janet: Has Alice finished reading *Moby Dick* **yet**?
Margaret: Yes, she has **already** finished it.
Janet: Well, Mark hasn't started reading it **yet**.

Outros advérbios usados no ***Present Perfect*** são ***already*** e ***yet***. Usamos ***already*** em frases afirmativas e interrogativas. Em afirmações, pode ser traduzido como "já" e aparece entre ***have*** ou ***has*** e o verbo principal. Essa palavra aparece geralmente no final de perguntas e expressa surpresa por algo ter acontecido. Usamos ***yet***, por sua vez, na interrogativa e na negativa, no final da pergunta e da frase. Na interrogativa, pode ser traduzido como "já" e, na negativa, como "ainda".

Agora faça as atividades 7 e 8.

Word pop-up

to achieve – alcançar
to be better off – estar em melhor situação
grim – tristes
to handle – lidar
increase – aumento
leadership – liderança
power-sharing – divisão do poder
uptick – um pequeno aumento
feeling – sensação

1 Look at the picture and write sentences using the Present Perfect.

a. dust the furniture (✓)

He has dusted the furniture.

b. vacuum the carpet (✓)

c. make the bed (X)

d. tidy up the study room (X)

e. do the laundry (✓)

f. take out the trash (X)

2 Use the prompts to write sentences in the Present Perfect.

a. Sally and Jack / pick up the clutter (X)

Sally and Jack haven't picked up the clutter.

b. I / wash the dishes (✓)

c. My parents / clean the kitchen (✓)

d. Lucas and I / water the plants (X)

e. Grandpa / cooked dinner (✓)

f. Doug / sweep the floor (X)

3 Write these verbs in the Past Participle form.

a. to do done

b. to keep

c. to take

d. to make

e. to see

f. to fall

g. to give

h. to know

4 Read the dialogue and underline the correct verb form.

Mrs. Silva: Melissa, **have you cleaned/did you cleaned** your bedroom?

Melissa: Yes, I have. I **dusted/have dusted** the furniture when I woke up and I **have swept/swept** the room when I arrived from school.

Mrs. Silva: Great. Can you help me prepare lunch then? Check the recipe, please.

Melissa: All right. **Do you buy/Have you bought** ham and cheese?

Mrs. Silva: What ham and cheese? Oh, … for the lasagna! No, I **haven't bought/didn't buy** them.

Melissa: Mom!

Mrs. Silva: I **prepared/have prepared** some meatballs yesterday. Let's have meatballs instead.

Melissa: Again?

5 Look at the pictures. Then circle the correct answer.

a. He hasn't folded the clothes yet.
b. He has already folded the clothes.

a. They haven't finished painting the wall yet.
b. They have already finished painting the wall.

a. I have already washed the dishes.
b. I haven't washed the dishes yet.

6 Unscramble the words to form questions. Then answer them.

a. Japanese food / have / eaten / you / ever / ?

Have you ever eaten Japanese food?

b. Have / prepared / you / lunch / ever / ?

c. London / best friend / been to / ever / has / your / ?

7 Complete the sentences with *already* or *yet*.

a. They haven't finished washing the dishes yet.

b. Vivian has ________ picked up the trash.

c. Suzanne hasn't ironed the clothes ________.

d. Jonathan has ________ had dinner.

e. He hasn't arrived home ________.

f. My mom hasn't started shopping ________.

8 Write sentences about you.

I have already	I haven't... yet.

iCan

Check (✓) the box that best describes your performance in this unit.

1. I can talk about events at an indefinite time in the past. ☐ Yes, I can. ☐ Not sure.
2. I can talk about chores and responsibilities at home. ☐ Yes, I can. ☐ Not sure.
3. I can talk about actions at a definite and an indefinite time in the past. ☐ Yes, I can. ☐ Not sure.
4. I can use *yet* and *already* to talk about an indefinite time in the past. ☐ Yes, I can. ☐ Not sure.

PRESENT PERFECT: *JUST*

Check this out!
Christine has **just** uploaded a new photo.

Usamos o ***Present Perfect*** para expressar ações e estados no passado, mas que tenham relação com o presente.

O advérbio ***just*** reforça essa ideia, indicando que algo acabou de acontecer. Ele é usado sempre entre os auxiliares ***have*** ou ***has*** e o verbo principal no particípio passado (***Past Participle***).

Agora faça as atividades 1, 2 e 3.

PRESENT PERFECT: *SINCE* AND *FOR*

Tricia has had her video camera **for** <u>five years</u>.

Tricia has had her video camera **since** <u>2013</u>.

> ***Since* vs. *For***
>
> *since* = **beginning** of an action
> *for* = **duration** of an action

Como você já viu, empregamos o ***Present Perfect***, dentre outras possibilidades, para indicar ações e estados que se iniciaram no passado, mas ainda continuam a ocorrer.

Nesse contexto, usamos as palavras ***since*** e ***for***. ***Since*** sinaliza o início da ação, enquanto ***for*** expressa a duração de uma ação.

Agora faça as atividades 4, 5 e 6.

SIMPLE PRESENT VS. PRESENT PERFECT

The research **shows** the profiles of cell phone users around the world.
According to research, the number of cell phone users around the world **has increased** <u>since 2012</u>.

Em inglês, usamos o ***Simple Present*** para expressar fatos e eventos no presente.

O ***Present Perfect***, por sua vez, indica que um evento ou um fato se iniciou no passado, porém ainda não terminou. Empregamos esse tempo verbal para expressar a duração (com ***for***) e/ou o início (com ***since***) desse tipo de fato ou de acontecimento, mas não o seu fim.

Agora faça a atividade 7.

TOO AND *ENOUGH*

Alice's bedroom is **too** <u>messy</u>.

We need another pizza. This one is <u>not big</u> **enough**.

> ***Too* and *Enough***
>
> *too* = **more than necessary** (expresses exaggeration)
> *enough* = **a sufficient amount**

Em inglês, usamos os advérbios ***too*** e ***enough*** com adjetivos mas também com advérbios.
Too indica que determinada qualidade existe em demasia, com exagero. Essa palavra é usada antes de adjetivos.
Enough, por sua vez, transmite a ideia de que algo é suficiente. Esse advérbio é usado depois de adjetivos.
Agora faça a atividade 8.

Word pop-up

ever-increasing – sempre crescendo
figures – números
whereas – enquanto que
beneath – abaixo
about to – prestes a
judged – julgado
candid – franco
garnered – passado de *to garner*, conquistou
tween – pré-adolescente
engaging – envolvente
even – empatados
huge – enorme
ordinariness – normalidade
passionate – apaixonada
prominent – importantes
relatable – relacionável

1 Unscramble the words to form sentences. Then match them with the correct picture.

a. been / approved / have / Stella and Mary / for a scholarship / just

Stella and Mary have just been approved for a scholarship.

b. have / about our favorite actor / we / some shocking news / just / read

c. a selfie / Laura and Tina / have / just / taken

d. downloaded / she / just / has / a video

a

2 Use the verbs in the Present Perfect and add *just* to the sentences to say what people have done.

a. Peter's boss has just sent him an e-mail about the conference. (to send)

b. I ______ a new tablet. (to buy)

c. We ______ a lesson online. (to watch)

d. Dad ______ to say he will be late. (to text)

3 Now answer the questions below using *just*.

a. Have you watched Zack's new video yet? (✓)

b. Have you printed your homework yet? (✓)

c. Have you created a Twitter account yet? (✓)

4 Write the phrases in the correct column.

last Monday | five days | 10 a.m. | I was 12 years old | ~~Christmas~~ | a month | a long time | 2016 | ~~more than ten minutes~~ | breakfast | many days | a decade | we started school

FOR	SINCE
more than ten minutes	Christmas

5 Use some of the phrases from Activity 4 to write sentences about you in the Present Perfect.

a.

b.

c.

d.

6 Circle *for* or *since* to complete the sentences correctly.

a. I have watched streaming videos **for**/**since** the last 2 hours.

b. Larry has recorded a lot of videos for his YouTube channel **for**/**since** 2017.

c. Johnny has watched a lot of movies on his cell phone **for**/**since** he was 11 years old.

d. I have had a tablet **for**/**since** 5 years.

e. Sabrina has sent text messages **for**/**since** she was in middle school.

f. Tyson has listened to podcasts **for**/**since** the past few years.

g. Larissa and Amanda have taken a lot of selfies **for**/**since** they got a cell phone.

h. My mom has used her Facebook account **for**/**since** she was 25 years old.

7 Read the text. Then answer T (true) or F (false).

The State of the World's Children is a report into an extraordinary subject that affects almost every aspect of life for millions of children and adults around the world: digital technology. Because the influence of digital technology – and especially the Internet – has increased, the debate about its impact has grown louder: Is it a boon to humankind, offering unlimited benefit for communication and commerce, learning, and free expression? Or is it a threat to our way of life, damaging the social fabric, even the political order, and threatening our well-being? This is an interesting but essentially academic debate. Because for better and for worse, digital technology is a fact of our lives. Irreversibly.

Children using a tablet in Myanmar

a. The impact of the Internet hasn't changed. T F

b. Digital technology has affected only the lives of the adults. T F

c. Digital technology has positive and negative effects on people's lives. T F

8 Circle the correct options to form sentences.

a.

That	exercise	are	too	difficult.
Those	activity	is	enough	too.

b.

She	is	too	small	much.
This chair	don't	has	enough	for me.

c.

This	have	fast	enough	to get her on time.
They	aren't	too	cook	to stay.

iCan

Check (✓) the box that best describes your performance in this unit.

1. I can talk about actions that happened in the past, but are close to the present. ☐ Yes, I can. ☐ Not sure.

2. I can use time expressions to refer to the beginning or duration of an action. ☐ Yes, I can. ☐ Not sure.

3. I can use both the Simple Present and the Present Perfect. ☐ Yes, I can. ☐ Not sure.

4. I can use the adverbs *too* and *enough*. ☐ Yes, I can. ☐ Not sure.

Great things about growing old.

PRESENT PERFECT

We **had** many great experiences over the years.
We **have ridden** our bikes four times this week.

É muito comum usar o ***Present Perfect*** para expressar ações e estados que aconteceram em um passado não determinado ou que ainda se estendem até o presente.

Importante:
- com o ***Present Perfect***, usamos expressões de tempo que sinalizam a duração de uma ação, como as compostas por ***over*** (de que são exemplos ***over the years/months/weeks***) e ***for*** (***for years/decades***);
- nesse tempo verbal, podem aparecer também expressões que marcam o início, mas não o fim de uma ação, como ***this month/year***, desde que o período de tempo para que ela ocorra ainda não tenha terminado e ainda seja possível que o evento ou a ação indicada aconteça) e ***so far*** (que significa "até agora").

Agora faça as atividades 1, 2 e 3.

REFLEXIVE PRONOUNS

Ms. Harrison has taught **herself** how to play chess.
She is very proud of **herself**.

Reflexive Pronouns

I	→	myself	it	→	itself
you	→	yourself	you	→	yourselves
he	→	himself	we	→	ourselves
she	→	herself	they	→	themselves

Usamos os *pronomes reflexivos* (***reflexive pronouns***) quando o agente e o alvo da ação são os mesmos, ou ainda quando enfatizamos que o próprio sujeito fez algo, no sentido de "mesmo".

Agora faça as atividades 4 e 5.

ADVERBS OF MANNER

Alex reads really **fast**.
Alex was quite angry at her dog, but she cleaned up **fast**.

Adverb Formation

Adverbs that end in -ly			Adverbs with the same form as adjectives		
conscious	→	consciously	hard	→	hard
brilliant	→	brilliantly	right	→	right
			fast	→	fast

Usamos os ***adverbs of manner*** para indicar a maneira como algo é feito ou ocorre.

Essas palavras nunca vão para o plural. Elas se referem ao verbo e aparecem nas seguintes posições:
- imediatamente depois do verbo;
- depois do complemento do verbo, quando este exige um.

Importante:
- Formamos muitos dos ***adverbs of manner*** acrescentando ***-ly*** aos adjetivos, como em ***beautifully*** e ***sadly***.
- Quando o adjetivo termina em consoante + ***-y***, tiramos a última letra e acrescentamos ***-ily*** para formar o ***adverb***, como em ***noisy*** – ***noisily***.
- Os advérbios de intensidade (***degree adverbs***) são usados antes de adjetivos e advérbios e intensificam (ou suavizam) o sentido do termo a que se referem. São exemplos desse tipo de advérbio as palavras ***very*** (que quer dizer "muito"), ***really*** (que significa "realmente") e ***quite*** (que tem o sentido aproximado de "relativamente").

Agora faça as atividades 6, 7 e 8.

Word pop-up

to dabble – explorar, interessar-se
to depict – retratar
to feature – apresentar
grief – dor, sofrimento
nearby – próxima(o)
to seek (sought) – buscar
self-taught – autodidata
to beat – derrotar
to boost – estimular
bowel – intestino
breast – mama
decline – declínio, queda
mood – humor
prescription – receita médica
schemes – programas

1 Look at the information about Pete and Samya. Then answer the questions.

	 Pete	 Samya

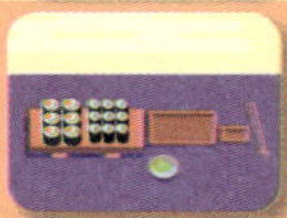		

a. Who has sung karaoke? Pete

b. Who has eaten sushi? ______

c. Who has traveled to New York? ______

d. Who has ridden a bike to school? ______

e. Who has read a lot of books? ______

2 Look at the table again. Then choose the correct options.

a. Has Pete learned to play the electric guitar?

(Yes, he has.) No, he hasn't.

b. Has Pete learned to swim?

Yes, he has. No, he hasn't.

c. Has Samya run a marathon?

Yes, she has. No, she hasn't.

3 Complete with the verbs from the box. Use the Present Perfect.

to buy	to receive	to lose	to break
~~to be~~	to ring	to play	to spend

a. This has been a great year for me.

b. The alarm clock ________ for 30 minutes straight.

c. My parents ________ a new apartment.

d. Cathie and I ________ five days at the beach.

e. My teacher ________ an award for her work at school.

f. I ________ my arm.

g. We ________ video games all day.

h. Laura ________ the spelling bee contest.

4 Circle the correct Relative Pronoun.

a. Joe and Patrick hurt **themselves/yourselves** during the soccer game.

b. I did the project **myself/ourselves**.

c. We enjoyed **myself/ourselves** at the birthday party.

d. Alexander cut his hair **themselves/himself**.

e. Monica prepared the Thanksgiving dinner **herself/himself**.

f. Don't do that! You're going to hurt **yourself/herself**.

5 Rewrite the sentences using a Reflexive Pronoun.

a. Barbara made the cake. She didn't have any help.

Barbara made the cake herself.

b. Riley and I planned the presentation together. Just the two of us.

____

c. Simone, Thiago, and Ana worked on the art project without any help from their friends.

____

d. Fabricio told me the news. Nobody else said anything about it.

____

6 Complete with the correct adverb.

a. happy happily.
b. fast ______
c. hard ______
d. good ______
e. beautiful ______
f. quiet ______
g. patient ______
h. bad ______

7 Write sentences about you using some of the adverbs from Activity 6. Follow the example.

a. I had the conversation with my friend happily.
b. ______
c. ______
d. ______
e. ______

8 Complete the sentences with the adverbs from the box.

calm slow easy
brave correct ~~careful~~

a. The boy opened the box carefully to see what was inside.
b. I answered the quiz ______. I got 10 out of 10!
c. He approached the dog ______ so that it didn't run away.
d. Beth did all the gym activities ______. She's very fit.
e. The child stood up ______ after falling down.
f. Grandpa spoke to all of us ______. He's so patient!

iCan

Check (✓) the box that best describes your performance in this unit.

1. I can talk about actions that have not finished yet. ☐ Yes, I can. ☐ Not sure.
2. I can use Reflexive Pronouns. ☐ Yes, I can. ☐ Not sure.
3. I can express how people do things. ☐ Yes, I can. ☐ Not sure.
4. I can understand the differences between some adverbs. ☐ Yes, I can. ☐ Not sure.

I had just read a horror story.

PAST PERFECT

I **had just read** a horror story.

I **had watched** two horror movies with my sister by the time Mom got home.

1st action — 2nd action

Usamos o ***Past Perfect*** para falar de ações e acontecimentos que ocorreram em um passado anterior a outro evento ou ação também no passado.

Em frases formadas com esse tempo verbal, é muito comum o uso também do ***Simple Past***, que indica a ação ou o evento que ocorreu depois do que foi expresso pelo ***Past Perfect***.

Para formar o ***Past Perfect***, usamos a seguinte estrutura: sujeito + ***had*** + **verbo principal no *Past Participle***.

Importante:

É necessário prestar atenção às expressões temporais comumente usadas com o ***Past Perfect***. Algumas delas são:

- ***by the time***: tem o sentido equivalente a "no momento em que" e aparece antes da ação ou do acontecimento indicado pelo ***Simple Past***;
- ***after***: significa "depois" e vem antes da ação ou do evento indicado com o ***Past Perfect***;
- ***before***: pode ser traduzido por "antes" ou "antes de" e é posicionada antes da ação ou do acontecimento indicado pelo ***Simple Past***.

Agora faça as atividades 1 e 2.

PAST PERFECT: QUESTIONS

A: **Had** you **seen** a black cat in the tree before we talked last night?
B: No, **I hadn't**.
A: Really? What **had you seen**?
B: I **had seen** a black bird.

Yes/No Questions

Had	I	**done** it?
	you	**done** it?
	he	**done** it?
	she	**done** it?
	it	**done** it?
	you	**done** it?
	we	**done** it?
	they	**done** it?

Short Answers

Yes, **I had**.
No, **I hadn't**.

Formar ***yes/no questions*** no ***Past Perfect*** é muito simples. Basta invertermos a ordem entre ***had*** e o sujeito.

Para formar ***questions with question words***, precisamos inserir a ***question- word*** no início da pergunta. O restante da estrutura fica igual à das ***yes/no questions***.

Importante:

- devemos responder às ***yes/no questions*** com ***short answers***, apenas com o verbo auxiliar ***had*** ou a forma negativa contraída ***hadn't***.

Agora faça as atividades 3, 4 e 5.

ADVERBS OF FREQUENCY AND MANNER

Jordan **always** reads.

He is **usually** in the library after school.

He also writes very **quickly**.

He creates two horror tales **every month**.

Os advérbios de frequência (***frequency adverbs***) são usados para indicar quão frequentemente ocorre um evento ou uma ação. Eles aparecem depois do verbo ***to be*** e antes dos outros verbos.

As expressões que indicam frequência e são formadas por mais de uma palavra vêm, geralmente, no final da frase.

Os advérbios de modo (***adverbs of manner***) também aparecem depois do verbo principal ou do objeto (quando o verbo exige um).

Agora faça a atividade 6.

SENSORY VERBS + LIKE

A: Oh, **your perfume smells like candy! It's really nice, Jenny**.
B: Thank you, Carol! And how do I look?
A: You **look like** a princess.
B: I actually **feel like** one.

Utilizamos verbos relativos aos sentidos para falar sobre o cheiro, o sabor, a aparência, o som ou a sensação que algo tem. Normalmente, esses verbos – ***smell***, ***taste***, ***look***, ***sound*** ou ***feel*** – vêm seguidos de ***like***.

Agora faça a atividade 7.

Word pop-up

balcony – varanda
in disguise – disfarçados
love at first sight – amor à primeira vista
poison – veneno
priest – padre
recognizes – reconhece
tomb – túmulo

1 Read the information about Charlie's life. Then write sentences using the Past Perfect.

a. learned to skateboard – get a job

He had learned to skateboard before he got a job.

b. learn to skateboard – graduate from college

c. get married – learned to ride a bike

d. get a job – get married

2 Read the story. Then complete it with the verbs in the box. Use the Past Participle.

to wait	to spend	~~to leave~~	to look for	to ask	to recognize	to enter

"... so the woman (1) had left the room when Jack arrived. His friends told him she (2) ______ the whole party asking questions about him. A girl told him that the woman was blonde and was wearing a red dress. Another one told him that she was wearing a blue dress. Who was she? By the time the living room door opened, Jack (3) ______ everyone about the mysterious woman. He looked again; two women (4) ______ the room. Jack (5) ______ for that moment since he got to the party. He looked at them again. The two women had the same face, the same hair, but different color clothes. He (6) ______ them at first, but then he noticed something familiar. The two women who (7) ______ Jack the whole party were his twin teachers! They just wanted to congratulate him for passing the national exam."

3 Match the questions to the answers.

a. Had the teacher explained this before?

b. Had you read the spoilers before you watched the movie?

c. How many questions had you answered before the bell rang?

d. Had your sister left by the time your parents arrived home?

e. Why had she asked you about me?

f. Who had eaten the entire pizza before everyone arrived?

[ ] No, she hadn't.

[a] Yes, she had talked about this subject many times during class.

[ ] I'm not sure. I guess Tony had eaten it all.

[ ] Because she knows you are in my English class.

[ ] Yes, I had. I was curious to find out more about the story.

[ ] I had already answered all of them.

4 Write dialogues for the prompts below. Use the Past Perfect.

a. she – visit (**X**)

A: [Had she visited] many houses before she bought this one?

B: [No, she hadn't].

b. you – eat (**X**)

A: [ ] the dessert before you ate the pasta?

B: [ ].

c. your brother – study (✔)

A: [ ] before he took the exam?

B: [ ].

d. you – be (**X**) / you – visit

A: [ ] to that mall before?

B: [ ]. It was my first time there.

5 Write the verbs in the past participle. Then find them in the wordsearch.

a. to break [broken]

b. to drive [ ]

c. to make [ ]

d. to be [ ]

e. to take [ ]

f. to give [ ]

B	S	N	A	G	H	X	Q	I	L	F	C	G	O
E	M	G	Z	U	B	N	Q	N	E	K	A	T	R
E	I	O	V	B	F	S	E	D	M	N	I	O	K
N	F	J	S	K	L	S	T	V	H	H	X	Q	Y
C	A	T	Q	A	U	M	A	T	I	A	M	D	O
X	J	F	G	I	V	E	N	I	I	R	A	G	I
S	D	L	P	T	C	E	U	G	H	R	D	F	J
B	R	O	K	E	N	E	E	O	T	U	E	E	O
L	B	C	K	M	V	I	T	E	F	A	S	B	M
B	X	M	M	I	G	F	I	D	Y	E	R	L	L

6 Check (✓) the correct answers about you. Then write complete sentences. Follow the example.

	every day	very often	once a month	usually	never
a. go to the movies			✓		
b. read print books					
c. post pictures online					
d. stream movies					
e. play a musical instrument					

a. I go to the movies once a month.

b. ____

c. ____

d. ____

e. ____

7 Complete the sentences using the sensory verbs below in the appropriate form.

to feel   to smell   to taste   ~~to look~~   to sound

1. You look like you've seen a ghost! Are you OK?
2. Did you turn off the oven? It ____ like something is burning.
3. Your homemade pasta is great, Henry! It really ____ like my mom's recipe.
4. I don't think I've ever been in love. What does it ____ like?
5. These neighbors are so noisy! It ____ like there is a band playing downstairs.

iCan

Check (✓) the box that best describes your performance in this unit.

1. I can talk about past actions. ☐ Yes, I can. ☐ Not sure.
2. I can identify which past action happened first. ☐ Yes, I can. ☐ Not sure.
3. I can use adverbs of frequency. ☐ Yes, I can. ☐ Not sure.
4. I can use adverbs of manner. ☐ Yes, I can. ☐ Not sure.

Moving away.

FIRST CONDITIONAL

If it snows in Paris, I will buy a thick coat.
present situation — future consequence

I will buy a thick coat if it snows in Paris.
future consequence — present situation

Usamos o ***First Conditional*** para falar de ações e acontecimentos no futuro que quase certamente ocorrerão caso se concretize certa condição no presente.

Esse condicional é formado pela ***main clause*** (oração principal) e pela ***if clause*** (oração subordinada que se inicia com ***if*** e expressa a condição para que algo aconteça).

No ***First Conditional***, a ***main clause*** apresenta o verbo com ***will*** e a ***if clause*** é formada com o ***Simple Present.***

Importante:
- se quisermos expressar determinada situação com menor grau de certeza, usamos ***might*** na ***main clause***;
- se a ***if clause*** começa a frase, usamos vírgula para separá-la da principal.

Agora faça as atividades 1, 2 e 3.

FIRST CONDITIONAL: *QUESTIONS*

If you go to Colombia, will you stay in Bogota?
Where will you go if you visit Bogota?

Para formar ***yes/no questions*** com o ***first conditional***, invertemos a ordem entre ***will*** e o sujeito.

Para compor ***wh- questions***, inserimos a ***question word*** no início da pergunta. O restante da estrutura fica igual à das ***yes/no questions***.

Na negativa e na interrogativa, se começamos a pergunta com a oração iniciada por ***if***, usamos vírgula para separá-la da ***main clause***;

Respondemos às ***yes/no questions*** com ***short answers***, apenas com o verbo auxiliar ***will*** ou a forma negativa contraída ***won't***.

Agora faça a atividade 4.

PREFIXES: ADDED TO THE BEGINNING OF THE WORD

Myles can be very **im**mature sometimes.

Prefixos são usados para formar palavras e são acrescentados ao início das palavras para alterar o significado dela.

Prefixes	Meanings	Examples
anti-	against	anti-hero
auto-	self	autobiography
co-	with	co-creation
dis-, in-	not	dissatisfied, inadequate
extra-	more than	extracurricular
mis-	wrongly	misbehavior
pre-	before	premeditated
re-	again	recreate
un-, im-, ir-	opposite	unwilling, immature, irresponsible
over-	too much	overbook

Agora faça as atividades 5 e 6.

SUFFIXES: ADDED TO THE END OF THE WORD

Jonathan is always respectful of his grandfather's ideas.

Suffixes	Meanings	Examples
-ence	state or condition	appearance
-er	person or object that does a specified action	driver
-ible	able to be	flexible
-ic	relating to, characterized by	specific
-ify, -fy	make or become	intensify
-ion	quality or state	assumption
-ness	quality or state (forms nouns)	happiness
-ship	skill of, state or condition of	scholarship

Os sufixos ***(suffixes)*** são acrescentados ao final das palavras para alterar o sentido delas. Certos sufixos podem fazer com que uma palavra passe para outra classe gramatical.

Agora faça as atividades 7 e 8.

Word pop-up

feasibility – viabilidade
novel-length – grande, de longa duração
venturing – aventurando
attainment – realização
flow – fluxo
income – renda
low-skilled – pouco qualificado
scholarship – bolsa de estudos
scope – âmbito
employee – empregado
employer – empregador
expat – expatriado, estrangeiro
field of work – campo de trabalho
researcher – pesquisador
split – divisão

1 Danilo is going to spend 3 months in the United States as an exchange student. Read the suggestions people gave him. Then write sentences using the First Conditional .

a. you don't go to be early – be late for school

If you don't go to bed early, you will be late for school.

b. you follow the GPS – not get lost

c. your host family has time – they take you on trips

d. you buy a lot of electronics – not have enough money for food

e. you don't buy winter clothes – be very cold

f. you study hard – pass the English test

2 Match the columns to form sentences.

a. I will miss soccer practice

b. If it rains,

c. If my brother passes his English exam,

d. The teacher will explain the topic again,

e. We'll go to the beach next weekend

f. If the bus doesn't arrive soon,

( ) if it's sunny.

(a) if I don't finish my homework.

( ) the school picnic will be canceled.

( ) we'll have to take a taxi to the party.

( ) if everybody has questions about it.

( ) he will move to Canada with me.

3 Write sentences about you using the First Conditional. Follow the example.

a. have time — If I have time, I will take dance classes.

b. have money

c. win a ticket to...

d. have Wi-Fi connection

4 Complete the questions and answers. Use the First Conditional.

a. **A:** What will you eat if you are hungry during the movie? (to eat)

B: I will probably eat popcorn. (to eat)

b. **A:** ______ you ______ me if you decide to go to the club? (to call)

B: Of course! I ______ you right away. (to call)

c. **A:** If I ______ with you, will you feel sad? (not to go)

B: No, I ______. Don't worry about it. I know you're busy.

d. **A:** What ______ you ______ if you arrive home early? (to watch)

B: I ______ the new episode of my favorite TV series. (to watch)

5 Find the opposite of the words below in the word search.

happy possible clear patient expensive polite satisfied honest lucky correct

V	J	S	V	N	B	U	D	B	H	Q	O	F	V	P	G	O	E	Z	B	I
K	P	O	Y	D	I	K	B	Q	I	N	E	X	P	E	N	S	I	V	E	M
E	T	C	E	R	R	O	C	N	I	Y	X	R	K	O	M	Q	E	N	A	P
Y	D	E	I	F	S	I	T	A	S	S	I	D	Q	X	D	P	P	Y	B	A
Z	V	V	N	M	J	S	L	O	R	D	I	S	H	O	N	E	S	T	O	T
Y	K	C	U	L	N	U	F	U	M	X	P	E	O	K	G	Y	G	T	J	I
J	G	O	C	O	U	N	H	A	P	P	Y	H	R	A	E	L	C	N	U	E
D	C	X	X	C	M	Y	S	Y	R	K	O	M	Q	E	N	A	T	M	K	N
R	I	M	P	O	S	S	I	B	L	E	P	E	T	I	L	O	P	M	I	T

6 Complete the sentences with the correct prefix.

1. Nory doesn't have many friends at school. She is very un popular.

a. dis **b.** un

2. You don't have to feel ______ secure about your first day at high school. You're going to be just fine!

a. ir **b.** in

3. I don't know where my cell phone is. It has ______ appeared.

a. dis **b.** un

4. Tanya is so ______ respectful to everyone. She's always rude!

a. dis **b.** im

7 Circle the suffixes and write the words in the correct column:

difference happiness direction membership creation conference
actor teacher election correction kindness assistance sadness relationship friendship

-ence, -ance	-er, -or	ion	-ness	-ship
difference				

8 Use the words from the box to complete the sentences.

dangerous horrible wonderful painful editor furious

a. The editor is responsible for correcting the text before the book is printed.

b. I had never seen my mom like that. She was ______ about the mess the dog made in the living room.

c. My brother had to go to the dentist. He had a ______ toothache.

d. We had a ______ time at the beach. It was sunny and hot.

e. Be careful! Don't go to the edge of the mountain. It's ______.

f. Is it ______ when you do that exercise?

iCan

Check (✓) the box that best describes your performance in this unit.

1. I can use the First Conditional to talk about possible future situations.	☐ Yes, I can.	☐ Not sure.
2. I can use the First Conditional to ask about possible future situations.	☐ Yes, I can.	☐ Not sure.
3. I can use *prefixes*.	☐ Yes, I can.	☐ Not sure.
4. I can use *suffixes*.	☐ Yes, I can.	☐ Not sure.

If I had one wish...

SECOND CONDITIONAL

If I could have any superpower, I would fly.
hypothetical situation — consequence

I would fly if I could have any superpower.
consequence — hypothetical situation

Usamos o ***Second Conditional*** para falar de ações, situações e acontecimentos irreais, hipotéticos que ocorreriam caso se concretizasse certa condição.

Esse condicional é formado pela ***main clause*** (oração principal) e pela ***if clause*** (oração subordinada que se inicia com ***if*** e expressa a condição para que algo aconteça).

No ***Second Conditional***, a ***main clause*** apresenta ***would*** + verbo na ***base form***. E a ***if clause*** é formada o ***Simple Past***.

Note que:

- as formas contraídas de ***would*** são "***'d***" na afirmativa e "***'d not***" ou "***wouldn't***" na negativa;
- se a ***if clause*** começa a frase, usamos vírgula para separá-la da principal;
- no ***Second Conditional***, usamos a forma ***were*** do verbo ***to be*** para todas as pessoas na ***if clause***.

Agora faça as atividades 1 e 2.

SECOND CONDITIONAL: QUESTIONS

A: If you could travel today, would you go to Portugal?

B: No, I wouldn't.

A: **Where** would you go?

B: I'd go to Thailand.

Em ***yes/no questions*** com o ***Second Conditional***, a oração com ***would*** vai para a interrogativa. Assim, invertemos a ordem entre ***would*** e o sujeito. A oração com ***if*** fica igual à afirmativa ou à negativa.

No caso das ***wh- questions***, inserimos a ***wh- word*** no início da pergunta. O restante da pergunta fica igual às ***yes/no questions***.

Importante:

- se começarmos a pergunta com a oração iniciada por ***if***, usamos vírgula para separá-la da ***main clause***;
- geralmente respondemos às ***yes/no questions*** com ***short answers***, apenas com o verbo auxiliar ***would*** ou a forma negativa contraída ***wouldn't***.

Agora faça as atividades 3 e 4.

FIRST CONDITIONAL VS. SECOND CONDITIONAL

If I **have** time this weekend, I **will do** volunteer work.
If I **were** a millionaire, I **would travel** to a different place every day.

O ***First Conditional*** expressa situações possíveis e prováveis que acontecerão no futuro caso determinada condição se concretize.

O ***Second Conditional***, em contrapartida, expressa situações irreais ou que pouco provavelmente aconteceriam, pois a condição para tanto está distante da realidade.

Agora faça a atividade 5.

TAG QUESTIONS

Marshall **will go** surfing tomorrow, **won't he**?

Negative	Affirmative
He likes it, **doesn't he**?	He doesn't like it, **does he**?
You are happy, **aren't you**?	You aren't happy, **are you**?
She will do it, **won't she**?	She won't do it, **will she**?
Lisa was going to take the bus, **wasn't she**?	Lisa wasn't going to take the bus, **was she**?
Dad washed the dishes, **didn't he**?	Dad didn't wash the dishes, **did he**?
They have cleaned it, **haven't they**?	They haven't cleaned it, **have they**?

Tag questions são perguntas que fazemos para confirmar alguma informação. Elas sempre sucedem uma oração (na afirmativa ou na negativa) e são formadas apenas com o verbo que seria usado para fazer uma ***yes/no question***, com essa sentença seguida do pronome que substituiria o sujeito dela.

Importante:

- se a sentença está na afirmativa, a ***tag question*** fica na negativa; se a sentença está na negativa, a ***tag question*** fica na afirmativa;
- nas ***tag questions*** negativas, usamos as formas contraídas do verbo.

Agora faça a atividade 6.

Word pop-up

indeed – de fato
unless – a menos que
eager – ávido(a)
envision – antever
approach – abordagem
geothermal and hydropower sources – fontes geotérmicas e hidrelétricas
heat – calor
mayor – prefeito
rail – trilho de metro ou trem
proud – orgulhosos
release – publicar
thought-provoking – estimulante

1 **Read this news article. Then complete it with the Second Conditional.**

Children were asked what they would do **(to do) if they** were **(to be) Prime Minister of their countries.**

A group of children were asked what they ______ (to do) if they ______ (to be) Prime Minister of their countries. Leaders around the world should take note of their great answers!

One child said he ______ (to feed) the poor. Another promised he ______ (to eliminate) all types of violence and guarantee that people coexist peacefully. Another child said she ______ (to construct) homes for animals, street children, and beggars. Some wanted to promote women's safety, and many desired and stressed universal education. Many listed the environment as the top priority. A young boy said he ______ (to reduce) carbon footprints. Another child's goal was to ensure there was less noise and less pollution. One child's wish was more practical. He declared he ______ (to build) sanitary facilities like toilets in every home.

2 **Write sentences. Follow the example.**

a. (I / clean the rivers / be / mayor of my city)

I would clean the rivers if I were the mayor of my city.

b. (I / build more subway stations / be / the governor)

______

c. (We / end poverty / have / that kind of power)

______

d. (My teacher / build more schools / have / the money)

______

e. (That candidate / give free meals at school / be / elected)

______

f. (Suzy / declare world peace / be / the president)

______

3 Write dialogues for the prompts below.

a. buy a private jet (**X**) buy a helicopter (✔)

A: If you won the lottery, would you buy a private jet?

B: No, I wouldn't.

A: Then what would you buy?

B: I would buy a helicopter.

b. go to school by train (**X**) go to school by bus (✔)

A: ______ if you moved to another neighborhood?

B: No, I ______.

A: Then how ______?

B: I ______.

c. play soccer (**X**) play video games (✔)

A: ______ if you didn't have to study for the test?

B: No, I ______.

A: Then what ______?

B: I ______.

d. build more hospitals (**X**) build more schools (✔)

A: If she won the election, ______ ______?

B: No, she ______.

A: Then what ______?

B: She ______.

e. go to work by bike (**X**) go to work on foot (✔)

A: If they had time, ______ ______?

B: No, they ______.

A: Then how ______?

B: They ______.

4 Now write sentences about you.

What would you do if…?

a. you were the mayor of your city?

b. you were the principal of your school?

c. didn't have any homework?

d. could modify your neighborhood?

5 Decide whether the situations are POSSIBLE or HYPOTHETICAL and write them in the correct column.

Where would you go if you could fly?
I would revisit my childhood if I had a time machine.
I will watch my favorite TV series if I arrive home early.
Patrick will cock dinner for us if he has time.
Would you live on a desert island if you had the money to buy one?
We will be late for school if we don't take the bus.
What would you do if you won the lottery?

POSSIBLE	HYPOTHETICAL
I will watch my favorite TV series if I arrive home early.	

6 Match the questions to the correct tags.

a. You were there,
b. Sam didn't come to class yesterday,
c. You can speak Spanish,
d. Bruna won't move to another country,
e. She wouldn't do that to us,
f. Katy and Paul are married,
g. Anna is your sister,
h. Daniel has broken his arm,
i. The students aren't late,
j. The boys played basketball yesterday,

( ) would she?
( ) are they?
( ) did he?
(a) weren't you?
( ) hasn't he?
( ) will she?
( ) didn't they?
( ) aren't they?
( ) can't you?
( ) isn't she?

iCan

Check (✓) the box that best describes your performance in this unit.

1. I can talk about hypothetical situations.	☐ Yes, I can.	☐ Not sure.
2. I can use the Second Conditional.	☐ Yes, I can.	☐ Not sure.
3. I can talk about real and unreal situations using conditional sentences.	☐ Yes, I can.	☐ Not sure.
4. I can use Tag Questions to confirm information.	☐ Yes, I can.	☐ Not sure.

Building healthy relationships.

RELATIVE PRONOUNS

Family is a circle of people **who** love and support each other through thick and thin.

relative clauses

Friendship is a bond **which** provides a sense of belonging and support.

relative clause

Relative Pronouns

who: used for people **which:** used for things	**that:** used for people and things

As ***Relative Clauses*** (equivalentes às orações subordinadas adjetivas em português) têm valor de adjetivo. Usamos essas orações para explicar ou especificar o sentido do termo ao qual nos referimos.

Elas são introduzidas por um pronome relativo (***Relative Pronoun***), que retoma um termo da oração principal e evita, assim, repetições.

Importante:

- ***that*** pode ser usado para retomar tanto palavras que designam objetos, ações etc. quanto palavras que designam pessoas.

Agora faça as atividades 1 e 2.

RELATIVE CLAUSES

Writing is a powerful tool **that** can be used to express emotions, share ideas, and inspire change.

subject

The novel **that** people enjoy the most explores themes of identity and belonging.

object

Os pronomes relativos podem exercer duas funções nas ***relative clauses***: sujeito e objeto. Para identificar a função desses pronomes, podemos substituí-los pelos termos que eles retomam.

Quando o pronome relativo tem a função de objeto, ele pode ser omitido sem prejuízo ao sentido da frase.

Agora faça a atividade 3.

BE GOING TO VS. *WILL* (REVIEW)

A: Next year, I'**m going to move** to Denver.
B: I'**ll miss** you.
A: I'**ll miss** you, too.

Empregamos tanto ***will*** quanto ***be going to*** para tratar de eventos futuros. No entanto, preste atenção à diferença de sentido entre eles.

Usamos ***will*** para expressar uma decisão que tomamos no momento da fala, uma previsão ou uma promessa.

Quando empregamos ***be going to***, expressamos uma ação planejada, indicamos maior grau de certeza de que algo acontecerá ou destacamos que temos intenção de fazer algo.

Agora faça as atividades 4 e 5.

PRESENT CONTINUOUS: FUTURE ARRANGEMENTS

They **are making** a presentation next week.

Além de ***be going to*** e ***will***, usamos o ***Present Continuous*** para expressar ações e eventos futuros.

No entanto, utilizamos esse tempo verbal para expressar apenas ações que foram planejadas e que certamente ocorrerão.

Agora faça as atividades 6 e 7.

Word pop-up

demanding – exigente
prevent – prevenir, impedir
tools – ferramentas
rats (gíria) – diacho
regardless – independentemente

1 Read the quotes and circle the correct relative pronoun.

a. The communication skills **that / who** we develop in relationships are essential for understanding each other.

b. People **who/which** prioritize personal growth contribute positively to their relationships.

c. A friend **who/which** listens attentively creates a safe space for open communication.

d. Trust is a foundation **that/who** supports every healthy relationship.

e. A crucial component of a healthy relationship is empathy, **who/which** is the ability to understand and share the feelings of others.

2 Join the two sentences using *who* or *which*.

a. I saw the woman. She left a message.

I saw the woman who left a message.

b. We didn't do well in the competition. It was disappointing.

c. I didn't get any messages today. It is unusual.

d. The woman is wearing blue. She is my mother.

e. Do you know the boy? He is talking to Pedro.

f. Tanya couldn't answer the question. It surprised me.

3 Check (✓) if *that* can be omitted in the sentences.

a. Where is the book <u>that</u> I gave you? ✓

b. I haven't listened to all the songs <u>that</u> I downloaded. ☐

c. The girl <u>that</u> is talking on the phone is Vivian's sister. ☐

d. Bryan loved the video <u>that</u> you showed him. ☐

e. Did you find the picture <u>that</u> you were looking for? ☐

f. The woman <u>that</u> was talking to you is our new gym teacher. ☐

4 Match the two columns.

1. It's very windy and cold here.
2. What are your plans for next Sunday?
3. I'm thirsty.
4. What are you studying?
5. What would you like to eat?
6. Cell phones are like computers now.
7. These bags are heavy.
8. What is Stella doing during her vacation?

A. I'm going to visit my grandparents.

B. I think I'll have meatballs.

C. Spanish. I'm going to take a proficiency test tomorrow.

D. I'll help you carry them.

E. I'll close the windows and turn on the heater.

F. She's going to travel to Australia and spend a month there.

G. I agree. In the future there won't be desktop computers anymore.

H. I'll bring you some water.

1	2	3	4	5	6	7	8
E							

5 Complete the sentences using *will* or *be going to*. Make the necessary changes.

a. The phone is ringing. Don't worry. I [will] answer it. (✓)

b. My friends and I [ ] play chess tonight. (✓)

c. I [ ] Bella's party next week. I have to study for a test. (**X**)

d. I think you [ ] do great in the test. (✓)

e. We [ ] stay here in the rain because we can get sick. (**X**)

f. Kimmy [ ] go to the dentist this afternoon at 2 p.m. (✓)

6 Match the arrangements to the evidence.

a. We're having a party at our house tonight.

b. The students are visiting the Art Museum at 10:00 a.m.

c. Felipe is watching a movie this afternoon.

d. I am going to the dentist next Thursday.

e. I'm traveling to Argentina next week.

f. I am meeting a friend after school.

g. My father is cooking dinner tonight.

h. Clara is studying for a math test this afternoon.

7 What are your future plans? Write sentences using the Present Continuous for the future.

Today I am ______

Tomorrow at 10:00 a.m. I ______

Tomorrow at 8:00 p.m. I ______

Next weekend I ______

Next week I ______

iCan

Check (✓) the box that best describes your performance in this unit.

1. I can use Relative Clauses to talk about different topics.	☐ Yes, I can.	☐ Not sure.
2. I can talk about the future using *will/won't*.	☐ Yes, I can.	☐ Not sure.
3. I can talk about the future using *be going to*.	☐ Yes, I can.	☐ Not sure.
4. I can use the Present Continuous to talk about future arrangements.	☐ Yes, I can.	☐ Not sure.

Audioscripts

Unit 1
Uploading 4, page 17

I recently left a school where I was bullied and now I am being home schooled until the start of the new academic year, when I will move to a new school. My mom works very hard to look after me and my four siblings. My dad works long hours. I don't really have anyone to talk to because all of my siblings believe that I am being favored because I am being home schooled. I don't really connect with anyone of my friends as they are all shallow and love to talk about things like crushes and dating. I have no interest in this and find that I am often excluded when I meet up with them. I feel awful about myself. What should I do? Thanks!

Unit 2
iListen 1, page 38

Aunt Rosie: Hello.

Zac: Hi, Aunt Rosie. It's Zac.

Aunt Rosie: Oh, hi Zac. How are you doing?

Zac: I'm OK, and you?

Aunt Rosie: I'm fine… a bit tired because of the party.

Zac: Cathy's birthday party?

Aunt Rosie: Yes. I still have so many things to do.

Zac: Umm, so, Aunt Rosie. I need some extra money to go on a field trip next month. I was thinking I could help you with some chores…if you paid for the work. What do you say?

Aunt Rosie: Perfect. I really need some help.

When can you come?

Zac: Is tomorrow afternoon OK?

Aunt Rosie: That's fine! So… let's see… I can pay you 10 dollars for each chore. Is that OK?

Zac: Yeah, that's great!

Aunt Rosie: We have to clean the garage, give out the invitations, prepare the decorations, make hot dogs, set the tables, and get some soda at the store.

Unit 4
Uploading 3, page 67

a. **A:** Have you seen Johnny's new car? It's a BMW!

B: Wow! They're really expensive and fast!

b. **A:** Do you like my new tennis shoes?

B: Yeah! They're really nice. Were they very expensive?

A: No, not very.

c. **A:** Look! That is Gloria's new boyfriend.

B: Oh! He's very handsome.

d. **A:** Patricia is very smart, isn't she?

B: Yes, she is quite intelligent!

Unit 5
Loading 1, page 76

Something very scary happened last night. As you know, my parents and I are spending the weekend at my aunt's house on the beach. It was late. My parents had already gone to bed. The neighbors had already turned off the lights. Everything was silent outside. All I could hear was the waves on the beach. I had just read a horror story and was ready to go to bed. Suddenly, I heard a noise. I went to the living room and turned on the lights. I didn't notice anything different there. Then I heard the noise again. It came from the kitchen. I slowly walked into the kitchen and opened the door.

It was my aunt's cat. Guess what? She had eaten all the bananas my dad and I had bought in the morning. When I looked at her, she came over and rubbed up against my legs.

iListen 1, page 84

I had never seen such a beautiful place before I visited Paris last year. I had saved money for about two years before I booked the trip. I was very excited, because I had never been abroad before.

The city is really big, so I spent many days touring. Sometimes I got lost and asked for directions. I know how to speak French because I studied French for 2 years before I visited Paris. I had read a few books about the city two months before the trip and found out about a lot of places I would like to visit- it made me want to visit the city even more!

By the time I left Paris, I had visited many beautiful places. The Eiffel Tower, Notre Dame Cathedral, and Luxembourg Gardens were just a few.

Unit 6

Uploading 3, page 97

Lauren: So, Jonathan… how do you like your new city?

Jonathan: Well, it's OK. There are some problems though…

Lauren: Really?

Jonathan: First of all, I think I need some nice tips to make friends there. Nobody talks to me!

Lauren: Hmm… maybe you should talk to them. After all, you speak the same language!

Jonathan: Plus, getting to school in the morning is terrible. The subway is really, really crowded.

Lauren: Oh, that's too bad… I hate crowded subway trains. Can't your dad drive you to school?

Jonathan: It would be even worse! The traffic is awful! There are too many cars and too much pollution.

Lauren: And is the city clean?

Jonathan: No, it isn't. The streets are terrible! They're really dirty.

Lauren: I'm sorry to hear that, Jonathan… I hope I won't have those problems when I move abroad.

Jonathan: Well, if you move to this city, I will make sure you have a more pleasant experience and a lot more help than me.

Unit 7

Uploading 5 and 6, page 111

a. If I were the mayor, I would have guards in front of schools to help children cross the streets.

b. I would restrict food such as ice cream, pizza, some chocolate candies, and donuts in schools.

c. I'd make school lunches tastier.

d. If I were a mayor, I would fight cyber bullying.

e. I would improve the cycling conditions in the city.

f. I wouldn't invest too much in tourism if I were the mayor. I'd prefer to focus on the health care system.

g. I would make the school year shorter.

h. If I were the mayor, all restaurants and supermarkets would be pet-friendly!

Unit 8

iListen 1 and 2, page 128

Interviewer: How did you start making YouTube Videos? Why do you think this medium is best for your message?

YouTuber: I started making videos back in 2007, as a way to keep in touch with people while I was away at college. It was perfect for me because I could talk into a camera, show things around my dorm room, and introduce my high school friends and family to my college friends. Nearly a decade later, I could never have imagined it would turn into what it is now.

Interviewer: You share so much of yourself with your fans. What's something you think they don't know about you?

YouTuber: There's PLENTY they don't know about me! Being in charge of what I share is something I really have to remember and be conscious of while creating, and making sure some things are just for me is so important. And if I told you, then it wouldn't be for just me, would it?

Interviewer: As a kid, what did you want to be when you grew up?

YouTuber: I always thought I'd be a teacher! In fact, I went to school for it at Michigan State University, but it never ended up coming to fruition. In a way, YouTubers are kind of teachers. We have an opportunity to use our platform to share what we know with the world, and maybe get people to think a different way or see a different perspective.

Interviewer: What are three things you always bring when you are traveling?

YouTuber: A friend, an iPhone charger, and a pair of sweatpants.

Audio tracks

iLearn 4 Student's Book

Unit	section	page	track
	Copyright notice	-	1
Welcome	Loading #1	12	2
Welcome	Loading #3	12	3
1	Loading #1	16	4
1	Uploading #4	17	5
1	Loading #1	18	6
1	Loading #1	20	7
1	Loading #3	20	8
1	Loading #1	22	9
1	Loading #2	22	10
1	Reading Hub #2	136	11
2	Loading #1	30	12
2	Loading #3	30	13
2	Loading #1	32	14
2	Loading #1	34	15
2	Loading #3	34	16
2	Loading #1	36	17
2	Loading #3	36	18
2	iListen #1	38	19
3	Loading #1	46	20
3	Loading #1	48	21
4	Loading #1	60	22
4	Loading #1	62	23
4	Loading #4	62	24
4	Loading #2	64	25
4	Uploading #3	67	26
5	Loading #1	76	27

Unit	section	page	track
5	Loading #1	78	28
5	Loading #3	78	29
5	Loading #1	80	30
5	iListen #1	84	31
6	Loading #1	90	32
6	Loading #1	92	33
6	Loading #4	92	34
6	Loading #2	94	35
6	Uploading #3	97	36
6	English for Culture #2	99	37
7	Loading #1	106	38
7	Loading #2	106	39
7	Loading #1	108	40
7	Loading #3	108	41
7	Uploading #4	111	42
7	Uploading #5	111	43
7	Loading #1	112	44
7	Loading #2	112	45
8	Loading #1	120	46
8	Loading #1	122	47
8	Loading #1	124	48
8	Loading #3	124	49
8	Loading #1	126	50
8	Loading #3	126	51
8	iListen #1	128	52
8	iListen #2	128	53

Notes

Notes

Notes

Notes